RELIGION IN OUR SCHOOLS

RELIGION
IN OUR SCHOOLS

by
Philip R. May
and
O. Raymond Johnston

HODDER AND STOUGHTON

FOREWORD

by the Bishop of London

THERE is a growing concern about the place of religion in our
national system of education. The present statutory provisions
are being challenged by leading humanists, and there are
Christians also who are critical of the compulsory element
and who would wish to see the religious education of Christian
children made the responsibility of the Christian churches
alone. Yet all the evidence which can be obtained from public
opinion polls shows that the vast majority of parents wish
their children to have a Christian element in their education.

The issues are complex, yet they are the concern of the
whole nation. I welcome warmly, therefore, this work
Religion in our Schools which gives a balanced statement of the
justification of religious education in our State schools and,
at the same time, shows how much must be done to make
that religious education more effective.

The authors have written this work out of a wide knowledge
of education, and against the background of much practical
experience of teaching. What they have to say is important
and I hope that it will be read widely. Those who care for
religious education will find much sober encouragement.
Those who are critical of the present situation will find a
reasoned justification for the Christian concern for education
as a whole.

ROBERT LONDON

CONTENTS

INTRODUCTION

THERE is one textbook of which nearly every child in the land has a copy. That book is the Bible. It may be a school copy or a personal copy from home. It may be the version of 1611 or the Revised Standard Version At least once a week it is taken out to be read. The lesson may be called religious knowledge, or religious instruction, or scripture, or divinity. The significant fact, however, is that religious education is always timetabled. And it is there by law in every school week, the only subject which is prescribed by statute. Our purpose in this present work has been to explain the place of religious education in our state schools for the benefit of those outside the teaching profession who are interested in the aims and methods of such religious teaching. We offer what we consider to be a non-controversial statement of the reasons for the presence of religion in maintained schools and have tried to give a picture of what is involved in the job of religious education today. Public discussion is not always as well informed as it should be, and we hope that parents and others will find our book helpful. National concern about educational matters is increasing, and it is our hope that public interest in religious education will result in more widespread support for generous and imaginative planning by education authorities, governing bodies, colleges and university departments of education. Student readers thinking of teaching as a career will find here a sketch of what is involved in the teaching of scripture. Perhaps some of them may even consider joining the ranks of the teachers of religious knowledge. If they do so with their eyes open after reading this book, our labour will not have been in vain.

We should like to thank the large number of teachers who

have been good enough to share their experiences with us to enable us to write chapter four. In particular we are most grateful to Mr. T. Greener who has lectured for some years to students in both the Durham and Newcastle University Departments of Education and is at the same time head of the divinity department of a large grammar-technical school; we have been much helped by his wise counsel at all stages, and from his specialist knowledge and wide experience he has contributed most of the material for the chapter on content and methods.

Many of the problems that still remain in the field of religious education are writ large on the whole religious scene. If the Christian Church herself is divided (as she is) on precisely what is implied by the centrality of the Bible—which most Christians would be happy to assert in a general sense—then it is scarcely to be expected that there should be unanimity among religious educators. But we feel that one side of the debate has received disproportionate publicity in the last few years. This is hardly surprising after *Honest to God* and its aftermath. One of our aims in writing this book has been to restore the balance. Not all Christians will agree with everything in our own modest contribution. While we certainly do not believe that religious education is impossible without open Bibles on desks in every lesson, we are still convinced that all who teach religious knowledge, at whatever level, are in need of a source of religious truth by which to check their own thinking, their projects, and their new imaginative syllabuses. The finest schemes impeccably built out of 'life-themes', or problem centres, or open-ended discussions, can soon degenerate into sheer sentiment or the eloquent sharing of common ignorance unless (on the teacher's side, at any rate) a measuring rod is available. If there is such a thing as religious truth, then there must be an ultimate reference point. It is our conviction that the Bible remains the sole standard. The teacher who knows it and lives by it may not insist on its being always there on the desk, but his explanations of Christianity will have an authentic ring. We do not advocate any attempt to return to the 'magic book' stage, but we are convinced that religious education would lose its meaning and direction if our children never had the Bible before them. As we hope our readers will discover, the task of leading children to an intelligent understanding of this book is one of the most difficult yet rewarding in education today.

CHAPTER I

A Christian Country?

BOOKS, articles and discussions on the nature of society are common today, and very popular. Current trends are described, various aspects of society are subjected to particular scrutiny, and attempts are made to analyse its character, essence and quality of life. As a society we are today becoming much more self-conscious and critical. This is due in great measure to the nature of life with its peculiar pressures and demands, its greater haste and, most of all, its stress on change. We in the United Kingdom live in a highly industrialised society. One consequence of this fact of varied industrial development has been the gathering together of people, in ever increasing numbers, in towns and cities where industries are centred. Rural areas have been increasingly denuded whilst urban areas have continued to expand, a process which still continues unchecked. We enjoy virtually full employment, there is a tremendous variety of jobs, new industries are coming into being and some older ones are expanding rapidly. Prosperity is widespread. All these facts help to explain the increasing social mobility which is an obvious characteristic of our society now. Change is in evidence everywhere.

Compared with the inter-war period, the social climate of Britain in the second half of the twentieth century has altered noticeably. Relationships between the various groups in our society have become much more complex than they were fifty years ago. The old closely-knit traditional society with its clear divisions and boundaries had its generally accepted and understood authoritative ties and moral codes. These have largely gone. The rapid urbanisation and increased opportunities for social movement have had disruptive effects on family life and ties. The older community groupings have been weakened. Such factors have combined with the restless temper of the times to encourage the rise of individualism. Too many people live self-centred and therefore separate lives. The result is loneliness, and in some cases a ruthless pursuit of personal desires and advantage. Most of us enjoy more personal freedom now. Formerly accepted restraints and compulsions have been questioned and removed. Permissive attitudes are more common, especially in the upbringing of children. This is also true of attitudes in general to the behaviour of others in the community. At the same time, life has become for many much more fragmented. People are much more isolated than they were, work and leisure time have become less intimate and personal, and gone for the majority is that sense of security and belonging which was typical of the older traditional society.

It is with all this in mind that writers and speakers frequently contend that the people of the United Kingdom now live in an 'open' society. What is meant by this word 'open' is not always made clear, and it is possible to detect several meanings in the various contexts in which the word is used. Karl Popper defined the open society as "the society in which individuals are confronted with personal decisions".[1] The closed society for him is the magical or the tribal or the collectivist society, and indeed members of such communities were greatly restricted. They enjoyed stability but they had little or no freedom within their group, whilst life outside it was most difficult, and often impossible. Since our society is very different in character we can accept his definition as, in some

[1] *The Open Society and its Enemies* (4th edition, Routledge and Kegan Paul, 1962), p. 173.

measure at least, applicable to our community and way of life. But to suggest as some appear to do that we have no obligations besides those of an aggregate of individuals each with the right to decide for himself about all the major and minor issues of life, is a very different matter.

Because we live and work together we have to adopt policies and attitudes *as a nation*. On certain matters therefore, there are national commitments, decisions and standards which may be examined and contrasted with those of other countries. Thus we can evaluate a country's politics, economic system, and religious temper. What distinguishes our own country in these fields?

As a democratic society we choose to impose certain restrictions upon ourselves. Our elected representatives in Parliament pass laws to plan the nation's economy. We decide upon and are guided by laws of contract and business generally. We impose compulsory schooling from five to fifteen years (and probably to sixteen years from 1970) for our children, and accept censorship in certain forms of entertainment. We restrict working hours, the use of public services, the times for the opening and closing of shops and public houses, and so on. We hope to protect the weak and ensure that the advantages of a more organised community life are enjoyed by all its members. Man is indeed now free as he has never been before. He is, some say, 'man-come-of-age', the responsible arbiter of his own destiny, the fully mature adult of the 'post-Christian era'. In this country we are free to choose how we shall be governed, a freedom gained only after centuries of struggle. We are free to choose how we use our leisure time. We enjoy much more leisure than formerly, and possible ways of using it are much more varied for everyone. Likewise parents are largely free as regards the nurture and upbringing of their children. Society demands that they ensure a satisfactory education for the children, and any parents found guilty of

gross neglect and cruelty are punished. But concerning the inculcation of moral and spiritual values and of acceptable social standards, parents can teach their children or not as as they please.
The government we freely elect does not impose upon the nation
one particular set of religious beliefs and moral practice. But
are we as a nation completely 'open' concerning religious belief
and moral behaviour, as some have recently suggested?

We believe that our society is not completely 'open' on
religious and moral issues. Certainly some writers continue
to urge us to 'self-fulfilment' through personal decision and
action without reference to religious and moral restraints
imposed from outside ourselves. Erich Fromm, for instance,
argues that man "is ready to enjoy 'freedom to' ", having
gained his freedom *from* clerical and secular authorities, "freedom to be himself, to be productive, to be fully awake."[1] It
is difficult to accept this as true in a welfare state which,
whilst happily enjoying freedom from such former problems
as fear, poverty and widespread unemployment, yet so cushions
most of its members that increasing numbers are abdicating
from some of their responsibilities as parents and citizens.

Evidence of this disturbing increase in social irresponsibility
can be seen in the following facts. Divorces granted in England
and Wales only, in 1962 totalled well over 28,000. In the five-
year period 1958–1962 the percentage increase was almost
28%. Also in 1962 nearly 81,000 people were convicted of
drunkenness, and the percentage increase over the same five-
year period was 29.5%. The crime rate also rose sharply, the
percentage increase over the five years being 27.5% for persons
found guilty of all offences. Particularly disquieting are the
steadily growing figures of those convicted of crimes of violence
and of sexual offences. All these figures continue to increase.[2]

1 *The Sane Society* (Routledge and Kegan Paul, 1963), p. 355.
2 For further details and comment on this aspect of contemporary life see O. R.
Johnston "Morality and Society Today" in *Faith and Thought* (Victoria Institute,
London, 1966).

In industry, unofficial strikes, which frequently cause many innocent people to lose their jobs, each year cost the country millions in lost man-hours, production and money. In home life more and more parents are looking to the schools to discipline their children, teach them good manners, and train them in moral responsibility, claiming that such tasks are not theirs but the schools'. These facts, a sample from many, cast serious doubt upon the claims that man is now adult, and able to exercise his freedom in responsible ways. But social irresponsibility does not prove that agreed national standards and attitudes have disappeared.

The view is sometimes expressed that the Christian claims must not now predominate because our society has become 'multi-belief', and Christianity is only one of many religions practised in this country. This may certainly be true of London, but is by no means the case for the country as a whole. T. S. Eliot commented that "the great majority of people are neither one thing nor the other, but are living in a no-man's land . . ."[1] Many would agree with this and with H. F. R. Catherwood that "the Christian Church has a diminishing impact on society" today.[2] Once a Christian nation, yes, but now, it is said, with the apparent absence of general commitment, with the growth of other religious groups, and with the rise also of agnostic humanism, really a neutral society.

This is a powerful argument. It derives particular force from the fact that though once we were a church-going community, over 80% of the populace no longer attend regularly at Sunday services. Most people appear indifferent to organised religion and turn a deaf ear to the pleas of all denominations to return to the pews. They have certainly largely rejected what they think organised churches stand for. This does not prove that they have completely rejected Christianity or that they, and

---

[1] *The Idea of a Christian Society* (Faber, 1939), p. 49.
[2] *The Christian in Industrial Society*, (Tyndale Press, 1964), p. xi.

2

therefore society also, are now neutral in religious matters.
In fact as the report *Television and Religion*[1] pointed out in
1964, only 8% of men and 4% of women say they have no
religion. Few societies have ever achieved religious neutrality.
R. H. Tawney in his essay "A Note on Christianity and the
Social Order" commented that "since man, as known to
history, is a religious animal, the alternative to religion is
commonly not irreligion, but a counter-religion."[2]

It is true that Christianity teaches that neutrality in religion
is impossible for any individual. Created in the image of God,
man is religious in very essence and fence-sitting is out of the
question. "He that is not with me is against me," said Christ,
and at the deepest level every individual must decide which
way he will go. But since the life of a nation contains underlying
standards and values which may be seen in attitudes and institutions, there is clearly a sense in which we can speak of a
Christian country also. The term 'Christian' in this context
will not be taken to imply that every individual or even the
majority of individuals is committed to faith in Christ in the
deepest sense. The term will be used to describe a nation
which clearly rests its observable attitudes and social behaviour
upon Christian values. The United Kingdom's official stand
is still definitely Christian, and the terms 'neutral' and 'open'
may not at present be applied to our society as a whole.

There is another relevant argument here. This concerns the
suggestion, frequently stated by some, that religious belief is
something personal and private only, and has nothing to do
with society as a whole. A. R. Vidler describes this view as
holding that "the state was properly concerned with temporal
welfare and material interests also. Religion was concerned
with spiritual and other-worldly interests."[3] Thus, those who
hold to this idea say that it is ridiculous to conceive of society

[1] University of London Press, 1964, p. 9.
[2] *The Attack and other Papers*, (Allen and Unwin, 1953), p. 191.
[3] *The Orb and the Cross*, (S.P.C.K., 1945), p. 21.

in religious terms, to describe it as Christian. It is true that, compared with the past, there is today less detailed and outspoken expression of Christian comment about the major aspects of our economic, social, and political life where biblical teaching is relevant to these. Nor do Christians when engaged in such dialogue always speak with one voice. This may encourage the belief that religion has no concern at the public level with the work, leisure-time pursuits and general communal activities of society. Christians at once reply, with adherents of other faiths also, that religious conviction and its practical outworking has never been entirely a private affair. In fact Christianity has never ceased in one way and another to influence the social, political and economic development of the nation. It is vitally concerned with the whole process of living; not merely the personal devotions and collective worship of believers, but life in all its everyday aspects and occurrences. We continue to recognise this in the practice of many of our institutions.

The National Structure

Nations today have clear commitments to religions and to secular dogmas. We would refer to Marxist Russia, Buddhist Burma and Muslim Syria as examples. For most of its history the United Kingdom has been fairly described, both by its own people and by the members of the other nations of the world, as a Christian country. Most people would still so describe it, meaning by this that the laws, customs and general feelings of the people reflect a Christian outlook, and that at the national level at least, Great Britian upholds and acknowledges the beliefs and practice of Christianity. This is of course a weaker sense of the term 'Christian' than when it is applied to an individual, but its validity cannot be denied if we are prepared to use parallel terms of other nations where such countries have a national commitment to a particular religion or ideology.

However, when the Church preaches the Christian gospel, she must not allow any individual man to imagine that by virtue of his birth he is already a Christian in the deeper sense. There is no truly Christian individual without repentance and faith in the heart. But the idea of a 'godly nation' appears very clearly in the Old Testament even though at many periods in its history the nation of Israel contained only a minority of those who truly served the Lord with heart, soul, mind and strength. Religious adjectives may be used of communities and are so used in Scripture without implying that all constituent individuals are fully committed believers. As long as the two senses are kept distinct, both may validly be used.

At pivotal points in the social structure, our main institutions are specifically geared to Christian practices. The monarchy is a most obvious instance. Since the Elizabethan Settlement, the English monarch has been designated the supreme governor of the Church of England, and the Revolution Settlement of 1689 laid down that he or she must be a Protestant. Consider the title of our present queen. She is "Her Most Excellent Majesty Elizabeth the Second, by the grace of God, of the United Kingdom of Great Britian and Northern Ireland, and of Her other Realms and Territories, Queen, Head of the Commonwealth, Defender of the Faith, Sovereign of the British Orders of Knighthood". The national anthem is worded as a prayer to God. When a new monarch is anointed and crowned, at a great religious service in Westminster Abbey, he or she is reminded by the Archbishop of the divinely given nature of the office of monarch, and that prayers will be said every day in the Church for both the monarch and his or her ministers.

National government and the legal system also proclaim the fact that this is officially a Christian country. At the commencement of each new Parliament, every M.P. swears the oath of allegiance, that he or she "will be faithful and bear true alle-

giance to Her Majesty, Queen Elizabeth, her heirs
cessors, according to law, so help me God'',[1] though
may abstain from the oath on conscience grounds, and s.
affirm allegiance. Erskine May comments: "The ordinary f
and manner of administering and taking the oath are prescribe
by section 29 of the Oaths Act, 1909. Under this section the
person taking the oath holds the New Testament, or in the
case of a Jew, the Old Testament, in his uplifted hand and
says or repeats after the officer administering the oath the
words 'I swear by Almighty God that . . .' followed by the
words of the oath prescribed by law.''[2] When Parliament is in
session, each new day's business in both the Lords and the
Commons begins with prayers to Almighty God for wisdom,
direction and guidance "in all our consultations", asking Him
to grant that "the result of all our counsels may be to the
glory of thy blessed Name, the maintenance of true Religion
and justice", the welfare of monarch and realm and the
knitting of the hearts of all in true Christian love and charity.
Also it has long been the practice for the Commons to use St.
Margaret's Church, the Lords usually going to Westminster
Abbey, for thanksgiving and memorial services.

As the monarch is sworn in at his or her coronation, so
judges and magistrates swear to serve the king well and truly
and to do right to all. Each judge swears that he "will well
and truly serve our Sovereign . . . in (his) Office . . ." and
"will do right to all manner of people after the laws and usages
of this Realm without fear or favour, affection or ill-will, so
help me God.''[3] The opening of every new Assize begins with
a church service in which the judges dedicate themselves and
their work to God, seeking from the Supreme Judge of all
men, the power to uphold the law and rightly to administer it
for the benefit of all. Further, it is on the Bible that witnesses

[1] The Promissory Oaths Act, 1868, sections 2,10.
[2] *Parliamentary Practice*, (16th edition, Butterworth, 1957), pp. 288–9.
[3] The Promissory Oaths Act, 1868, section 4.

swear by Almighty God to tell the whole truth during court proceedings.

In the sphere of local government, mayor-making and other major ceremonies usually include an act of worship, and events such as Mayor's Sunday, or annual civic services of worship are held in many places. Members of the armed forces promise to do their duty to God and the monarch. At national events people flock to the churches, for instance when national days of prayer were proclaimed during the war, when victory celebrations took place, and at state funerals like those of King George VI and Sir Winston Churchill. Annual remembrance services to commemorate the dead of two world wars may also be cited. No other nation in the world continues these ceremonies. The fact of the Established Church speaks for itself in this context, and its parish system is by no means a dead organisation, although usually superseded now in local government and rendered obsolete as a community unit in some places by the practice of commuting. The Paul Report notes that "the fact of establishment is manifest to everyone in the crowning of kings and queens, in the bench of bishops in the Lords, in the magnificent cathedrals, in the special role of the Church in television and radio, and even in the attentiveness of the press to what bishops say and clergymen do."[1] There are numerous occasions in public life when God is acknowledged and sought out in prayer, like state banquets and certain national conferences. As the Paul Report noted, on the radio and on both B.B.C. and Independent Television religious services and programmes continue to be broadcast regularly, during the week as well as on Sundays. Religious broadcasts on the radio amount to roughly eight to nine hours per week, and on television nearly three hours per week.

The national education system is no exception either. The 1944 Education Act lays down that each school day shall begin

[1] Leslie Paul, *The Deployment and Payment of the Clergy* (C.I.O., 1964), p. 11.

with a collective act of worship, and that all children should have at least one period per week of religious instruction based on an Agreed Syllabus. Parents may withdraw their children from these activities, and teachers may similarly abstain on conscience grounds without prejudice to their careers. "It shall be the duty of the local education authority for every area, so far as their powers extend, to contribute towards the spiritual, moral, mental and physical development"(note the order!) "of the community by securing . . . efficient education. . . . to meet the needs of the population of their area", says the Act.[1] Most universities and colleges have their chaplains and grace before meals is the accepted practice in schools and university colleges and halls of residence. Lastly, the rhythm of the whole annual calender is that of the Christian year. Despite commercialisation, Christmas and Easter in particular are still public reminders built into the nation's life of the facts that Christianity proclaims.

At this juncture it may be objected that the religious observances referred to are in virtually every example merely part of an accepted ritual, having no real, live significance for the vast majority who are involved. The worship and the prayers were once sincerely heartfelt, it may be said, but only a small number so respond now. Nonetheless, this argument concludes, because we are a people who love tradition and ceremony, these aspects are retained since they have been part of the proceedings for so long. There is undoubtedly some truth in such comments. These outward institutional links with Christianity have nearly all been with us for four hundred years at least, many for centuries more, and they are integral parts of our history. Yet they have meaning for a larger number of people than is sometimes assumed. They undoubtedly acknowledge publicly that we are a nation under God, and there is no evidence to show that the people as a whole wish

[1] Ch. 31 Pt. II, 7.

to change this situation. Research has shown that more than 95% of those parents in the North East of England who replied to a questionnaire on religion in schools wanted their children to know about and understand Christianity. In a national survey almost 80% of those questioned said they regarded Britain as a Christian country.[1] This would certainly not be the case if we had ceased in *any* sense to be a Christian country. Thus, from only a brief look at the structure of our national life, there is clear evidence to support the contention that, in the eyes and to the satisfaction of the great majority of its members, the United Kingdom may justly be styled a Christian country.

National Standards

Further support for the view that ours is a Christian nation is found in a consideration of national standards, both legal and moral. A socially fluid society can expect that established material and moral values will be questioned, and that its attitudes to general social rules and activities considered worthwhile will be subjected to pressure for change. Attempts to make the law reflect more closely these new points of view will also be made. Alterations in the law usually lag behind changes in social codes and generally accepted social ideas, but the law at any given time is usually a fair expression of a nation's cultural outlook. In a very interesting book, *Law and the Laws*, Nathaniel Micklem asserted that "if proof be sought that England still remains to a large extent a Christian country, positive evidence could be afforded by the rules of public policy as recognised and enforced by law."[2]

From the time of Alfred, the long introduction to whose laws included translations of the Ten Commandments, passages from Exodus, and some apostolic history, Christian doctrine about man and his moral conduct has influenced English law.

---

[1] For further details of these surveys, see Appendix A.
[2] Sweet and Maxwell, 1952, p. 110.

This teaching is still reflected in many of its basic principles. There is the concept in common law of the free and lawful man[1] and the view that man is a responsible being, answerable for what he does or fails to do. Again, the belief in the sanctity of human life and the intrinsic worth of every individual which undergirds the Christian view of human equality, along with the principle of freedom of conscience, are central to legal thought and practice in this country. Christian marriage principles basic to our social structure and the belief in the sanctity of the home have helped to determine the law concerning family life and property. Lord Devlin has argued that Christian moral conviction is the basis of the criminal law. He asserts that "the law must base itself on Christian morals and to the limit of its ability enforce them, not simply because they are the morals of most of us, nor simply because they are morals which are taught by the established Church—on these points the law recognises the right to dissent—but for the compelling reason that without the help of Christian teaching the law will fail."[2] This links up with Micklem's view that "law as we have it is secure as long as Christian religious principles continue to be acknowledged."[3]

To argue thus is not to demand the legal enforcement of religious beliefs as determinants of behaviour in a society. This would only be justified if such beliefs were a condition of membership of that society. But the value and importance of Christian standards influencing the law, as is the case in this country, is more clearly seen when consideration is given to the law of a country which explicitly rejects Christianity. The civil code of the U.S.S.R., for instance, refuses to protect any rights which the state considers to conflict with the economic and social aims of the ruling proletariat. The individual in

[1] See Richard O'Sullivan's many references to this in *The Inheritance of the Common Law*, The Hamlyn Lectures, Second Series (Stevens and Sons, 1950), and *The Spirit of the Common Law* ed. B.A. Wortley, (Fowler Wright Books, 1965).
[2] *The Enforcement of Morals* (O.U.P., 1965), pp. 23, 25.
[3] *Op. cit.*, pp. 108–10.

Russia is subordinate to the state. Consequently the law is the tool of the government, not a protective shield for the individual citizen. There is no writ of *habeas corpus* in Russia. As Micklem said, "Freedom is always in jeopardy where loss of faith in God occurs" (and, we would add, where such faith has never existed)—"and that for two reasons, first because if there be no recognised jus divinum, there is no limit to the authority of the State; hence comes totalitarianism; second, because where man loses his sense of dependence on God, he loses his freedom over against the world, for there is for him no triumphing over the world by faith."[1]

In the generally accepted moral codes of the nation also, Christian ethical ideas predominate. The situation here has become much more complicated since the second world war, however. Expressions of uncertainty and confusion over moral assumptions and standards are quite common. All authority— of the Bible, of the state, of the law, of the family, of the teacher—is being questioned, and new 'authorities'—science, psychology, mass media, individual opinion—are being pressed as replacements for the traditional ones. Lawlessness is on the increase. Crime rates rise, the police are debunked, and established rules are flouted. There is much greater tolerance of variations in behaviour, and the balanced scriptural views of discipline and punishment are being replaced by more permissive attitudes, especially in the treatment of the young. Particularly widely publicised have been the opinions of the so-called 'new-moralists' who advocate situational ethics, a sort of morality of compassion not really based on any absolute values save that which they call 'love', a morality which has to be determined by each particular situation that arises. There is no real guidance here, nothing clear and tangible offered, and therefore such ethics are of little positive help, especially to the young and immature. In this situation the Church speaks

[1] *Op cit.*, p. 111.

with an uncertain sound, and at times with conflicting voices. As Harry Blamires said, the Church's abdication of authority in many spheres means that too often "prophetic condemnation of salient features of contemporary secularism comes nowadays from secularists."[1]

Nonetheless those voices which urge the rejection of traditional moral values in favour of self-pleasing, are very much a minority. Attempts, in literature and art, in 'pop' music, in drama, and in various television programmes, to put across values and moral behaviour which clash with the still generally accepted morality of society meet with much opposition and protest. We have not yet completely overdrawn at the bank of our spiritual heritage. People still regard New Testament ethics as the proper standard to be taught to the nation's children, and as the basis for social conduct in all walks of life. This is true of Christians and non-Christians alike. Bertrand Russell used to stress the importance at school and in society of Christian love and Christian morality, whilst rejecting the Christian faith. Many humanists today still desire Christian religious instruction to continue for all children at school, and base moral education on the ethics of the Sermon on the Mount. The "humanistic communitarianism, sharing *work*, sharing *experience*" which Erich Fromm claims is "our only alternative to the danger of robotism"[2] is recognisably influenced by Christian teaching. Christians and humanists, in other words, continue to agree on the second great commandment. The influence of nineteenth-century utilitarianism divorced this command from the first. Yet whilst Christians point out that obedience to the second follows from and depends on obedience to the first, non-Christians accept for themselves many New Testament principles of conduct. Any survey of mass opinion reveals that "the blend of custom and conviction, of

[1] *The Christian Mind* (S.P.C.K., 1964), p. 8.
[2] *Op. cit.*, p. 361.

reason and feeling, of experience and prejudice" which Dean
Rostow is quoted as saying makes up "the common morality
of a society",[1] is based on Christian belief and teaching. It
can be argued for these reasons that it is essential to our
national well-being that the Christian voice should continue
to educate opinion. There are powerful reasons for believing
that life must be kept as close as possible to the Christian
standards which the great majority of people still support.

Religious Behaviour

The current religious behaviour and opinions of people in
this country must also be considered. We have noted that the
majority are not regular churchgoers. It is nevertheless interesting and relevant to consider first some of the most
recently available facts concerning religious observance. The
Paul Report commented that "the Church is only surpassed
in audience figures by the organs of mass communication".[2]
The latest edition of the Church Information Office's "*Facts
and Figures concerning the Church of England*" (No. 3, 1965), gives
the following statistics. Infant baptisms in 1962 were 531 per
thousand live births, and 12,000 "persons of riper years" were
also baptised in that year. Numbers confirmed in 1964
amounted to 25.9 per thousand of the 12–20 year old population. Marriages solemnised in the church of England in 1964
totalled 474 per thousand, and more than four-fifths of the
total number of marriages in that year were religious ceremonies. By 30th June 1962, over 27 million of the population
were baptised persons (over 60 %), over 9.8 millions were
confirmed, and nearly 2.8 millions were numbered on Church
electoral rolls. Easter communicants totalled almost 2.16
millions, 69 per thousand of the population of fifteen years
and over. The Paul Report noted[3] that the number of confirmed

---

[1] *The Enforcement of Morals*, p. 95.
[2] *Op. cit.*, p. 27.
[3] *ibid.*, p. 26.

in 1960 exceeded the T.U.C. membership by over 1.5 millions and this was still true two years later. As Leslie Paul said, "Viewed religiously, the number of worshippers may be held to be unsatisfactory, but considered socially it is formidable and makes the Church of England by far and away the most important social institution in the land".[1] The Methodist Church annual report for 1964 gave the total estimated Methodist community in Great Britain as 2.1 millions, whilst Baptists and Congregationalists together number well over half a million. According to the Catholic Directory, January 1967, the Roman Catholic church in England has just over four million members. Anthony Sampson noted in 1962[2] that "since the war there has been an increase in the congregations in suburbs and new towns", a fact in line with Michael Argyle's comment that "there are indications of a general revival of religious activity since 1950."[3] It must be added that it is less certain that this activity continues as fully today, especially as many of the figures quoted above indicate a downward trend.

The influence of the Church in this country, however, continues to be extensive, a good illustration of this being its concern with youth. The Paul Report's claim that the Church of England is "easily the largest organiser of youth in the country",[4] still holds good. At the end of 1960, over one million children attended its Sunday Schools, which were run by 85,000 teachers.[5] The Methodist Church claimed in 1964 over half a million scholars, with an average attendance of almost 370,000. Anglican church youth organisations in December 1960, had a membership of nearly 295,000 in the age range 14–25 years, 211,000 of these being in the 14–17 age group. In addition, nearly 71,000 young people aged 14–20

[1] loc. cit.
[2] Anatomy of Britain (Hodder and Stoughton, 1962), p. 167.
[3] Religious Behaviour (Routledge and Kegan Paul, 1958), p. 25.
[4] Op. cit., p. 26.
[5] Facts and Figures Concerning the C. of E. No. 3, 1965.

were members of church-sponsored units of national voluntary youth organisations. The 1964 figures given for Methodist youth groups was over 105,000. Lastly, it is worth mentioning that in January 1963 the Church of England had almost 6,700 primary, 120 all-age, and 233 secondary schools, 7,046 in all out of a total of 9,579 non-county schools. Also, over 13,000 students attend church colleges of education, and these numbers will continue to increase.

The fact of Establishment is another illustration of the influence of the Church on national life and mores. It is a clear reminder to all that authority does not belong only to the State. It also helps to keep the State mindful of Christian values and standards, in two ways particularly: firstly, as regards the rights and needs of individuals; and secondly, in that the State itself is ordained by God to maintain order, reward virtue and restrain evil, and to uphold conditions in which the Church can worship freely and proclaim God's truth. It also follows from this, as William Temple once noted, that "the State must also see to it that the Church does not overstep its own proper function."[1] The Church has been at the centre of English life almost from the start, and it seeks still to be of service to all the nation. As A. R. Vidler has written, "the fact that the Church of England still has the framework of a national church, as distinguished from that of a gathered church, a sect or a religious denomination, is a constant reminder to its members and to the nation that it is inescapably involved with the whole of the society in which it is set."[2]

In concluding this section, some mention must be made of the widespread pro-religious attitudes still prevalent in this country. Of most obvious relevance to this book are the findings of recent national opinion polls concerning religion in school. Over 90% of those asked were satisfied with the present

---

[1] *Citizen and Churchman* (Eyre and Spottiswoode, 1941), p. 38.
[2] "Religion and the National Church" in *Soundings* (C.U.P., 1963), p. 257.

compulsory provisions regarding religious instruction and school worship. Our own research into parental attitudes to these provisions of the 1944 Act has revealed that this satisfaction is not mere indifferent contentment with the present situation, but a real concern based on definite reasons. And this concern is shared at all levels of the community. Enquiries amongst young people equally reveal, as the latest of these clearly shows, that whilst pupils may be anti-church, they are certainly not anti-religious. Indeed, J. W. Daines notes widespread goodwill towards religion in general.[1]

It does not follow from poor church attendances Sunday by Sunday, that the nation is now anti-religious or that people are no longer influenced by Christian teaching. Most people are very willing to call themselves Christian or pro-Christian if asked, and many, non-Christians included, are sincerely concerned that Christianity in this country appears on the surface to be institutionalised but little more. People may not seek out the churches as they once used to do, but they certainly buy religious publications. The Bible is still the world's number one best seller, and modern versions are extremely popular, as sales of the R.S.V., the N.E.B., and the J. B. Phillips' translation indicate. There is an undoubted boom in the sales of religious paperbacks, and other religious literature maintains steady sales.

Also for a so-called secular society, its people react in curious ways. The religious sense, a feeling for the numinous, reveals itself in many activities. The saying of grace at meals— local banquets, club dinners, private parties— is common, not out of respect for certain people present, but because it is considered the right and proper thing to do. Hymn singing at festivals, or at Wembley Stadium and Cardiff Arms Park is another interesting and always moving example. The wide-

---

[1] *Meaning or Muddle* (University of Nottingham Institute of Education Paper No. 5, April 1966), p. 40.

spread interest among all age-groups which has always been
shown in the Billy Graham evangelistic campaigns likewise
shows that pro-religious attitudes are extensive and ready to be
revealed, particularly when Christians are prepared to go outside their churches and speak in simple, forthright language
that anyone can understand. At all levels of society, respect
for Christian teaching and real concern for the maintainance of
Christian mores and values is generally professed. People may
not always put this teaching into practice in their own daily
lives but they recognise the biblical views on morality as the
standards at which to aim. Love, respect for others, honesty,
fair dealing, helpfulness, sympathy for and kindness towards
the less fortunate, self-control, these are some of the positive
Christian values which most people commend and desire their
children to learn and practice.

Conclusion

Enough has been said to demonstrate that ours is still a
Christian country in the sense that we earlier defined. The
nation as a whole continues to acknowledge one set of standards
as distinct from all others. The matter is well summed up by
T. S. Eliot who once wrote, "A society has not ceased to be
Christian until it has become positively something else."[1] He
contended that "we have today a culture which is mainly
negative but which, so far as it is positive, is still Christian."[2]
Every society needs the coherent view of life which religion
and Christianity supremely provides. And religious belief, to
extend a phrase of Lord Devlin's, is the main force behind the
morality of any society. God-honouring national institutions,
legal and moral codes largely based on Christian teaching and
insight, an education system which includes instruction in
biblical faith and ethics, and the free opportunities for regular

---

[1] *The Idea of a Christian Society* (Faber, 1939), p. 13.
[2] *loc. cit.*

worship enjoyed in this country, all together guarantee a national and social life which properly respects and values human personality, the rights of the individual, and the good of the whole community. A. R. Vidler stated that "the obligation of the State to concern itself with the moral and spiritual welfare of the whole people, and therefore with theological truth, is the corollary of its function to serve the well-being of the nation."[1] The alternative would be to resign society to the forces of self-interest and greed. This would be as R. H. Tawney said, "to de-Christianise both it and the individual souls whose attitudes and outlook are necessarily in large measure determined by the nature of their social environment."[2] Nor does it follow that justice and a proper respect and consideration for all are inevitable in civilised nations, as non-Christian societies from Plato's Greece to modern Russia and China show. To argue for complete neutralism, saying that nothing of religious and moral belief ought to be recommended to the individual is deliberately to try to destroy the source from which so much moral nourishment and social health has been channelled into our national life. It is as reprehensible as the idea of forcing everyone into one particular mould.

Perhaps the biggest cultural problem for this nation at present is that of communication. From the point of view of religion there is widespread ignorance of what the Christian message to the individual is about, nor have many in the Church yet learned (despite the excellent and successful work of some Christians) to express the gospel in understandable language. The real cements of a society are religion and language. These bind and unify a people as nothing else. They undergird society and remove the problem of isolation because together they both engender roots, stability, permanence,

---

[1] *The Orb and the Cross*, p. 73.
[2] *Op. cit.*, p. 176.

common values, a real sense of belonging, and personal, emotional ties. When both are effectively present, because generally shared and experienced with understanding, a real community spirit is not only possible; it is certain. Thus many see the most important of all the major tasks confronting educationists today as a twofold one. Firstly we must help all future citizens to communicate to one another with understanding. Secondly, we should assist them all to know about and understand Christianity. Then they may have something valuable to social well-being which they can communicate to their children and to the rest of the world. Christian teaching and the Christian perspective are vital in our children's education, and in our society as we have it today. Without them there is no guarantee at all that children will continue to be educated, or that people generally will continue to be treated, as human beings. Education, and in fact all national and social life, might easily degenerate for the majority into exploitation, the individual being completely subordinated to the dictates of the state, the ruling class, or the privileged few.

Enough evidence has been presented to demonstrate that the United Kingdom is still a Christian country. This assertion may be made with confidence provided we remember that the meaning of the word 'Christian' when applied to a nation is somewhat different from its meaning when applied to an individual. Great Britian is not a religiously neutral society, yet in Popper's sense it is open in that individuals are confronted with a vast range of personal decisions. It is clearly possible for a nation, without unduly prejudicing individual judgment, to uphold and commend Christian standards and practices; indeed most Christians and many non-Christians would maintain that it is essential for us to do so if we are to continue to enjoy the benefits of our society as we know it. It is equally possible at the same time to ensure the rights of every individual as regards personal opinion and responsible decision. One cannot force a person to be religious—to be a regular, active member of (in our case) the Christian Church. Nor does anyone desire to compel belief. But there is no warrant to abstain from putting before the nation, and especially before its children, one particular set of standards, Christian standards, standards which in any case are woven so inextricably into the whole fabric of our national life.

CHAPTER II

Why Religious Education?

ANY OBSERVER of the English educational scene who comes to
the study of our schools with knowledge of other systems is at
once struck by the way in which we have legislated for the
inclusion of religious teaching. This, as has often been
noted, is the one subject that *must* by law appear on the
timetable. This remarkable provision, which was scarcely
opposed at all when it was made a legal obligation in the mid-
forties, is now increasingly questioned. And the question
"Why religious education?" is not merely asking for an historical explanation of the present position. It is the more
urgent question demanding a public justification for the special
treatment of one subject in the contemporary scene. Are there
valid reasons today which support the case for the inclusion
of religious teaching to all children of compulsory school
age?

This question is not only being asked by hostile critics of
the Christian faith, though they are the vocal minority
whose voice is often heard.[1] The opposition of some
humanists and others to the inclusion of the subject in
the school timetable is well known, and has attracted considerable publicity. But the question is also being asked by
many who are by no means hostile to religion. This includes
both committed Christians and others who are without positive
religious faith, though well disposed towards it. Christians are

[1] See, for example, D. H. Tribe *Religion and Ethics in School* (National Secular
Society, 1965), 24pp.

beginning to wonder whether in all fairness they can support the provisions of the 1944 Education Act, which seem to many to date from some past 'age of faith'. Perhaps the churches are taking unfair advantage of the children of a new agnostic generation in retaining their entrenched position. Would it not be more honest and realistic to allow religion to disappear from the schools as it has already disappeared from the homes of so many citizens? In the face of these doubts it is clear that the reasons which have been advanced for the place of religious teaching in the schools need careful examination.

The first reason which has been given is what might be called the missionary motive. It urges that the task of school religious education is to produce Christians. This aim is a noble one in many ways, for it was the aim that first produced education for the people in most, if not all, European countries. The children must be taught to read so that they might read the scriptures and thus come to a knowledge of Jesus Christ. Any history of education will document the spiritual zeal which drove on the pioneers of education in our schools. It is scarcely surprising that those with the closest links with the past through institution and tradition, men like Anglican bishops, should sometimes have made pronouncements in favour of religious teaching in schools on the grounds that it produces good church members.

Nor is it possible to deny that many young people have considered and still do consider the teaching of scripture as a career because they see themselves as home missionaries, bringing Christian truth to the darkened minds of modern pagan children. The classroom to them affords an opportunity for evangelistic outreach. They point out that many children will hear the gospel in the scripture lesson who will otherwise never meet it. And there is little chance that the majority of them will ever go anywhere else where it is being proclaimed. Such a situation as this provides the challenge and the privilege of the religious education specialist. It is probable that an important minority of scripture teachers today still see themselves in this light, and often such devoted Christian staff make energetic and effective teachers.

Such an aim is further strengthened by the pronouncements of many Agreed Syllabuses. For instance, the county of Lincoln syllabus states that "the Syllabus is deliberately designed as an evangelistic instrument", and it goes on to state that "the aim is to lead the pupils to a personal knowledge of Jesus Christ and to active life within a worshipping community."[1] A fine end, born of most worthy motives. But it is seriously open to question in the present day. The only type of school in which it is still possible to maintain this position as the *raison d'etre* of the scripture lesson is the denominational school, be it independent or voluntary. In the case of the independent school the parent has chosen the school in the knowledge that it aims to bring up its pupils "according to the beliefs of the Church of England" (to take the most common example), or that it is a distinctively Methodist or Roman Catholic school. As far as the voluntary day schools are concerned, where the partnership with the local authority is closer, it is surely a delicate matter when the only school in a rural area is a church one. One would hope that, where the church had a monopoly of educational facilities, it would be judicious in its treatment of the religious instruction of children from homes where religious teaching was neither expected nor desired.

In the case of the fully maintained schools the position is quite clear. There are a number of powerful reasons for rejecting the missionary motive here. The first is the obvious matter of the captive congregation. It has never been the practice of Christianity in any but its most debased forms to propagate the faith to unwilling hearers by force. Apostles

[1] The quotations are taken from the 1964 edition, pp. 10—11.

and evangelists have gone to the crowds, or even assembled the crowds by their own magnetic oratory, but they have never used any kind of compulsion to assemble or retain their hearers. Yet children are at school because they have to be, and they cannot walk out if they do not like what they hear. If they are persuaded or directly appealed to in a way which might be perfectly legitimate in a church or chapel (to which a man goes of his own free will), most children will instinctively react unfavourably, however sincere their teacher. Their instinct here is surely right. Many thinking Christians today are seeing more clearly than before that this situation helps neither school nor church. The school should not be expected to produce specific religious conviction any more than it should be expected to produce political conviction. To blur the functions of church and school, of preacher and teacher, is to do a grave disservice to both institutions. The temptation to the zealous and energetic Christian teacher is greatest just here. His lessons can so easily become pulpit oratory. In a democratic society, unless the vast majority of citizens profess the Christian faith *and* have specifically entrusted the work of child evangelism to the schools, evangelism is not the function of religious education. Our own nation, as we have seen, is favourable towards the Christian religion, and wishes to see a close connection between the national life and the symbols, the ceremony and the morality of the faith. But this is very far from saying that the majority has specifically consigned the work of evangelism to the maintained school system. It is to be earnestly hoped that as Christians discuss amongst themselves and with others the problems of the religious education of our confused younger generations, they will make it clear that they neither desire nor expect to use the scripture lesson as a spearhead of Christian advance. The church must stand on its own feet. It is worth adding that much of the secularist opposition to religious education in the maintained schools springs from the belief that such teaching is specifically evangelistic in aim.[1]

The moral aim is one which commands widespread support. It is generally admitted that moral advance in our own society has largely (though by no means entirely) been due to the efforts of Christian individuals and groups, and that in general a religious belief gives a purpose in living and high, clear standards of conduct. Many of the parents who support the continuance of the 1944 legal obligation do so on specifically moral grounds, because it will give the children a better code of behaviour than they would otherwise have. The more thoughtful will agree that the highest and best of which human nature is capable is seen in the life of Jesus of Nazareth, and hence they see in Christianity the foundation of healthy moral values. So religious education is aimed at producing a sound morality. But there are serious defects in this as the main aim for the teaching of religion, even though it may well have loomed large in the minds of the framers of the 1944 Education Act as the nation emerged from its struggle with the evil powers of pagan despotism which ruled totalitarian Germany and Japan. No Christian will wish to deny that his is a faith which provides a great moral dynamic and a purgative influence against all that is evil in society. Yet the Christian believes what he believes because it is true, not merely because it is useful. There have been and there are today other creeds and philosophies that have provided liberalising and generous motives for individuals and groups. The beliefs of men like Ghandi and Dag Hammarskjöld are examples. The Christian does not wish to claim a monopoly of moral goodness for the adherents of his faith.

Many are asking today for more research into moral education and for the exploration of possible forms of moral training

---

[1] See, for example, Derek Wright "Ends and Means in Religious Education" in *Education for Teaching*, February, 1964.

divorced from religious belief, or at any rate from the traditional religious beliefs of our society. The Christian can have no objection to such investigations. There is no reason why he should not welcome the introduction of teaching about the ethical idealism of the other great world faiths. As Professor Hirst has pointed out,[1] orthodox Christianity maintains that men without revelation are capable of valid moral insights and judgments. Yet at the same time it must be stressed that no other system of belief can be compared with the Christian faith for its dynamic influence in the life of nations and of individuals. The separation of moral teaching from religion on anything but an experimental scale will only be justified when a comparable motivating creed has been found. Until then, the Christian makes no apology for advocating the retention of the close connection between morality and Christian faith in education.[2] The burden of proof lies upon the humanists and others to show a practicable alternative.

It would also be granted by most Christians that it is scarcely fair to teach Christianity, about which some of our fellow countrymen have their doubts, *solely in order to produce* good moral citizens, which the vast majority do want. Christianity must stand on its own feet as true if we are to teach it as undeniably true. If there are doubts, then let us teach it rather differently, and approach our moral education some other way.

Many Christian people would also add that they are unhappy to see their faith regarded as a convenient means to something else—a just and happy society. It is, to them, so much more than this that they find that religious teaching which has a primarily moral end in view tends to distort the whole biblical picture of what Christianity actually is. In fact, they would

[1] Paul H. Hirst, "Morals, Religion and the Maintained School" in the *British Journal of Educational Studies*, Vol. XIV, No. 1. November, 1965, pp. 5—18.
[2] For an elaboration of this point see P. R. May, "Moral Education and the Bible' in *Learning for Living*. Vol. VI. No. 2 November, 1966, pp. 10—12.

assert that the distinctively moral fervour of Christianity comes precisely from its specifically religious message.

Our position here must not be misunderstood. We do believe most emphatically that Christianity has contributed more than any other single influence to the refining of moral discrimination and the raising of moral standards. We have no doubt that an intelligent and broadly sympathetic approach to the study of the Christian faith cannot help contributing to the moral education of children. Religious knowledge lessons will inevitably face pupils both with the stories of men who made moral choices and with clear-cut ethical teaching. Yet to Christians, Christianity is more than a moral system, and it would be to distort the nature of the Christian faith to present it as merely a moral code.

On these grounds, then, both Christians and non-Christians would agree that to put the principal aim of religious education in school as the moral betterment of the child, or of society, is inadequate, however true it might be that moral health is in fact produced by religious faith.[1]

There are two further reasons which have been put forward for the continued presence of religious teaching in our schools, and they seem to the present writers to have far more weight as publicly justifiable aims, and also to be sound educational policy.

The first is what might be called the philosophical aim. As modern philosophers have studied the different ways in which men apprehend the world, they have constantly been faced with metaphysical beliefs. Man creates a system by which he structures the totality of his experience, he attempts to give a basic framework to all his thinking, a complete picture of the universe which he is always fashioning and re-fashioning for himself as he (the individual) grows and the accumulated knowledge of the race increases. The ultimate postulates of

---

[1] On this point, we agree substantially with Goldman in *Readiness for Religion* (Routledge and Kegan Paul, 1965), pp. 60–61.

this system are deeply felt—religious, in fact. This religious approach seems to be a special kind of apprehension, a particular way of looking at the world parallel to the artistic or aesthetic way and the scientific way. There seems to be a category of human experience called 'religious' and a particular type of language which accompanies it. R. S. Peters makes this point in discussing "education as initiation". Having noted that consciousness is the hallmark of mind, and that by the use of language the growing child learns to differentiate objects in the public world, Peters notes that in addition to the basic categories and concepts needed for objects in a space-time framework and for causal connections and means-ends relations, a further differentiation "opens the gates to a vast inheritance accumulated by those versed in more specific modes of thought and awareness such as science, history, mathematics, religious and aesthetic awareness, together with moral, prudential and technical forms of thought and action . . . The process of initiation into such modes of thought and awareness is the process of education."[1] Though answers to religious questions may often differ and the sense of religious language sometimes remains unclear, yet religion remains a fundamental facet of human life. And as such it is our duty to put it before children for them to "feel their way into" just as we do with aesthetic experience. As the Spens report stated as long ago as 1938, "no boy or girl can be counted as properly educated unless he or she has been made aware of the fact of the existence of a religious interpretation of life."[2] The most obvious, best-known and clear-cut body of religious tradition and experience is that of Christianity, and hence it is right and proper that there should be some study of it in our schools. All this may be asserted without pronouncing on the ultimate truth of Christianity or any other religion.

[1] *Ethics and Education* (Allen and Unwin, 1966) pp. 50–51.
[2] The Spens Report on Secondary Education (H.M.S.O., 1938) p. 208.

This brings us to our other aim, which again might well be agreed upon by both Christians and non-Christians. It is what might be termed the cultural justification for religious education. The fact is that it is quite impossible to understand the nature of our present society or of its past growth without some knowledge of the ideals and beliefs of leaders and movements of former times whose vision drove them to act in the way they did, and so to fashion what we now know. The laws of our land, its history and the constant flux of ideas which moulded public opinion down the centuries are unintelligible without some knowledge of the religion that enshrined the highest and best that our forefathers knew. The great works of art of the past—cathedrals, paintings, drama, poetry and music— have very often sprung from a Christian consciousness. Thus even if churchgoing were to continue to decline, the case for religious education in maintained schools would remain just as strong. It would even be admitted by many who do not profess the Christian faith that no such dynamic vision of life's challenge and of high ideals has arisen since the arrival of Christianity. No modern contender can replace the old faith. This is not to say that Christianity is true, or that it ought to be taught as such, but simply that children without a knowledge of what this faith is will be culturally impoverished. To deny children this knowledge is to deny them acquaintance with the richest part of their national heritage. Many thoughtful humanists agree that provided Christianity is not taught as a closed option ("Everyone believes it is true" or "Only fools reject it") it is important to give children a grasp of the stories upon which the faith rests and the kind of beliefs which Christians hold. As a group of Christians and humanists put it:

If genuine openness can be achieved, then we all agree from our different standpoints that the case for county schools continuing to undertake the task of religious education remains as strong as ever; not only do county school pupils need to be taught about the Christian religion as part of their cultural history, but it is right that they should also have the opportunity to share in an experience of the Christian religion as part of their total education.[1]

In rejecting the missionary and moral aims for religious education in schools it must not be thought that we would deny all validity to the religious and moral experience which comes out of such lessons, either directly or indirectly. As a later chapter will show, some of the most precious encouragements of the scripture teacher are those rare occasions when it does seem as if a real religious or moral commitment has been made by an individual pupil. Our point is that these experiences, if and when they occur, are essentially by-products. They are not the end towards which the teacher is directing all his energies. Neither Christian theology nor sound democratic procedure can justify these as the stated aims and purposes of school religious education. They are unrealistic, undemocratic and theologically unjustifiable grounds for the teaching of scripture in maintained schools.

Instead we suggest that the aim of religious education should be the understanding of the religious approach to life, and in particular a sympathetic insight into the Christian faith—the historical data on which it is based, its literature (chiefly the biblical material, obviously), its distinctive morality and its historical manifestations. All this can be taught in a genuinely open way so that no child is forced into any commitment to the Christian religion, but rather shown what it is that Christians profess and believe. Implied in this approach at all stages is the clear possibility of honest vocal rejection in discussion and debate. This means that there is no warrant

---

[1] *Religious and Moral Education*, by a group of Christians and Humanists, 1965, p. 2.

for the accusation that religious education in school is an attempt to impose the beliefs of a minority.

The teacher of religious knowledge is in the school to initiate into the cultural tradition just as much as is any other teacher. He is there to teach *about* Christianity rather than simply to teach Christianity. It is not unreasonable to hope for agreement from all sections of the community on this modest and realistic aim. If this is gained, then we have the public justification for the continuance of the present position, though some of our assumptions about methods of teaching may well need to be reviewed in the light of this modern formulation of our goal.

CHAPTER III

Objections to Religious Education

IN RECENT years there have been outspoken objections to the present position of religious education in maintained schools. Such attacks have increased in intensity, though this probably indicates an improvement in the organisation of the secularist minority rather than any marked increase in their numbers. But whatever their numerical strength, certainly their objections deserve some consideration, particularly since some of them have gained what many would judge to be a disproportionate amount of time on radio and television. The objections cluster round four main points.

1. *The privilege of the churches*

It has been objected that the religious clauses of the 1944 Education Act give to the churches an anomalous and unrepresentative position of privilege from which to exercise an undemocratic influence over the education of the nation's children. This objection may be answered quite briefly. We have in an earlier chapter maintained that ours is a Christian country. For this reason, to say that the school scene shows the churches to be in a position of privilege is to misconceive the whole situation. This objection attributes special and disproportionate influence to a minority group. But in fact it is the will of the whole nation which forms the basis of the case for special attention being paid to Christianity in schools. The vast majority of parents still desire their children to be taught about Christianity, and wish the schools to help in this teaching.

Furthermore, it should be made clear that religious instruction in maintained schools is expressly prohibited from being denominational. The daily act of worship and the religious teaching prescribed by the 1944 Act must not be distinctive of any particular denomination. If more ordained ministers of the various denominations take up positions as teachers of scripture in maintained schools, the situation may well demand further attention to this detailed requirement, particularly if these men have had no training as teachers. But in all other respects the situation is a perfectly clear and defensible one.

Religious education in school is not intended to do any more than help children to understand the nature of religious commitment and in particular what Christianity is. It is not aimed at making recruits for any church or churches. With very few exceptions those who teach it in the schools do not regard their task as agents, feelers or persuaders on behalf of outside bodies. They are undertaking a teaching task, albeit a difficult and taxing one, in accordance with the will of the nation. At present the British people have no wish either to dive or to drift into secularism. But the cry of "Churches' privilege!" is a red herring. Christianity is bigger than the churches, and to understand its teaching is not necessarily to accept it.

2. *The danger of hypocritical conformity*

The second objection to religious education in maintained schools is the assertion that the present legislation encourages hypocritical conformity in teachers and children. Both the teachers and their pupils, it is averred, are invited to pretend to believe what they do not in fact believe to be true.

Let us first consider the teachers, and begin by looking at the problem of attendance at the statutory morning assembly. Motives for attendance at the daily act of worship are many and various. The actual picture of teachers' motivation is a far more complex one than some would have us believe. The facile assumption that the key to the problem is simply the question "Religion—true or false?" is far from reality. There are many reasons for attendance at school worship. Some teachers attend from a sense of loyalty to the head teacher. Some see it as a *school* activity which they feel an obligation to support. Some will stress the communal value of the school's meeting together, whatever form the meeting may take. Others add that they see it as their duty to set the children a good example. Many teachers make the point that it seems unfair that the children are expected to be there if adults turn up casually or not at all so they come to assembly irrespective of personal belief. Though perhaps inadequate in some respects, all these motives show praiseworthy features, and it would be rash to dismiss them out of hand. They probably represent the main ingredients in the minds of most of those teachers who, though not themselves convinced Christians, do attend their school's morning assembly.

Some teachers may attend morning worship out of a mere desire to conform, and thus merit the charge of being hypocritical, though our impression is that these are far fewer than before the second world war. There may also be some who attend out of sheer ambition, concealing their considered rejection of the value and purpose of worship. One would hope that convinced secularists would not stoop to this level, but have the courage of their convictions. If they were to stay away on principle, their friends and colleagues would respect them all the more for this. Admittedly such a course of action is a handicap if a teacher aspires to become a head teacher. Though in some cases a head may prefer to ask a colleague to act as "chaplain' (perhaps this practice could be further encouraged), normally the head is expected to conduct morning worship. But in a Christian country with an educational system clearly and honestly geared to a national profession of the Christian faith, it is difficult to see how this

4

situation could be avoided. Even in a fully democratic society some individuals—those with beliefs which are not in harmony with those of the majority— are bound to be to some extent handicapped. This is inevitable in a society in which the majority wish to set and publicly maintain definite standards and values in the sphere of morals and religious belief.

It should be added too that the 1944 Act does make specific provision for teachers who have conscientious scruples. No teacher *need* take part in daily school worship or be required by the head teacher or anyone else to give religious knowledge lessons.

One other remark must be made about religious instruction. We concede that there seem to be real difficulties over the position in the primary school, where each class teacher is still expected to teach every subject (or almost every subject) to his or her class. Here we may note that many teachers do tackle biblical material with real professional skill and concern, though they do not profess themselves to be whole-hearted Christians. There is much that can be done by such teachers. Perhaps the best solution to aim for in the long term would be for the primary schools to have specialist teachers of scripture, rather in the same way as specialist teachers in French are becoming increasingly popular at this level. And here again we should not forget that legally the teacher's rights are protected by the act.

The charge of hypocrisy is sometimes levelled at the present position from the point of view of the pupils. We have already shown that attendance at religious knowledge lessons does not imply acceptance of the Christian faith by any of the pupils, nor does it require or expect such acceptance in the short or the long run. It is, however, in connection with daily school worship that the accusation of encouraging hypocrisy in children is most often levelled. In a later chapter we shall defend the morning assembly on broadly psychological and social grounds. We shall show also that much depends on the form and content of the assembly in a particular school. Here we would point out that in many schools a well conducted, reverent and effective morning assembly has always been a familiar part of each school day. Many head-teachers are successfully attempting new and flexible forms; others are modernising and streamlining older types of morning worship equally effectively. All these efforts are aimed at making worship meaningful and interesting to the children.

Here it must be stressed that parents may, if they wish, ask for their children to be withdrawn from assembly. This is their legal right. The remainder are expected to attend, but no belief is either demanded or expected of them. They may be encouraged to take part but they are not forced to do so. The saying of the Lord's Prayer and the "Amens' could not be universally demanded, even if such a demand were practically enforceable. No positive personal response from individual children is required, though clearly the opportunity for such is there. It should hardly need saying that this will be a response to God and not to the head or the staff, and as such it will in the majority of cases be unknown to those around. Its genuineness in respect of any particular child or any particular occasion will be beyond the bounds of verification. Worship is the setting and the opportunity, but no more.

In this connection we must stress that no suggestion is ever made that because the majority of children attend assembly, *therefore* all teachers or all adults expect them to be fully convinced believers. There is no hypocrisy here. Nobody is deceiving, nobody is pretending, and nobody is being taken in. Under these circumstances the charge of hypocrisy is wholly inappropriate.

3. *The spectre of 'fundamentalism'*

It has been suggested occasionally that because the Bible is the main item in school religious teaching, and because in the primary school at least most teachers are expected to give religious education irrespective of personal belief, a tendency to uncritical and literal teaching is inevitable. This tendency is broadly named 'fundamentalism' and deplored, since it is said to inhibit future development of religious thinking, and to prevent the conceptual refinement which is said to be the characteristic of adult belief.

There are several points to be made in answer to this objection. Firstly, it must be granted that in so far as *all* childish thinking is unrefined, lacking in subtlety and perspective, certainly it will be difficult and probably impossible to prevent children from adopting rough-and-ready, crude concepts in their apprehension of religious truth. This happens in all subjects — mathematics, science, history, geography and so on. General truths are enunciated in the primary school which are later qualified. Wider perspectives and deeper knowledge, as well as greater linguistic mastery and more experience of the world, all contribute towards maturer thinking. The good primary teacher is fully conscious of the fact that he or she is simplifying issues dozens of times a day across the whole range of subjects taught. Very often such teachers have to do this for any clear impression to be made at all. The whole field of children's development in religious thinking (as in other areas) is at present under review, and no firm findings in this field command wide agreement. Certainly the matter is not as simple as those who use this objection are prone to assume.

But this particular criticism must also be examined from the teacher's stand-point, and from the theological angle. On closer examination, we find that in many respects the word 'fundamentalism' makes discussion more rather than less difficult. What *is* fundamentalism? Is it superstitious reverence for the text of the Authorised Version of the Bible? Is it literal interpretation of the whole Bible? Is it in principle antiscientific, or irrational in some other way? These problems were fully debated in two books by Anglican theologians A. G. Hebert and J. I. Packer, published in 1957 and 1958 respectively.[1] The latter writer suggested that the term 'fundamentalism' should be dropped, as it confused genuine theological discussion. Our own inclination would be to agree with this suggestion.

The real question here is that of authority in the Christian religion. What is the purest source of Christian truth, and to what or to whom ought the Christian church to refer in order to settle religious questions and differences? The answer given by the mainstream of historic Christian thinking clearly points to an authoritative Bible. There is no doubt that this was the position of Jesus and His apostles, who saw the Old Testament Scriptures as God's word written. The classic Protestant position is that the New Testament completes the written revelation by which the Church was meant to live and govern herself. Certain traditions within Christendom have invested men or groups of men with kinds of authority equal to that of the Bible (the 'catholic' tradition), whilst others have taken it upon themselves to stand in judgment over Scripture and accept only those portions of the Bible which commend themselves to their own critical scrutiny (the 'liberal' approach). Historic Protestantism preserves the stress on Scripture alone, and accepts the whole of Scripture as normative. Each of these three approaches has a long history. As Dr. Packer showed, 'fundamentalist' is the twentieth-century smear term used by some 'liberal' and 'catholic' thinkers to refer to the third more conservative group. The more recent post-war 'biblical theology' movement attempts to hold a position somewhere between the liberal and the classical reformed positions, and has had considerable influence.

---

[1] See A. G. Hebert *Fundamentalism and the Church of God* (S.C.M. Press, 1957) and J. I. Packer *"Fundamentalism and the Word of God"* (I.V.F., 1958).

We do not wish to deny that there is such a thing as 'ignorant literalism' in the approach to the Bible, or that this very occasionally finds its way into the schools. But as a dogmatic attitude it would seem to be fostered only by such groups as Jehovah's Witnesses who are quite outside the stream of historic Christian belief. But few teachers, if any, come from these quarters. 'Fundamentalist' is far more often used of orthodox Christians from within the main denominations who have inspected the liberal criticism of the Bible and the theological radicalism which enjoys a certain vogue today, and found them wanting. Teachers who are theologically conservative in their thinking have nothing to apologise for. There is no evidence that the more conservative approach of teachers who regard the Bible as a trustworthy guide inhibits or impedes children's religious development. Rather the contrary.

It is not our purpose to go further into the matter here, but enough has been said, we hope, to show the reader that there is a point for reasoned discussion, a matter of theological debate at a high level, not for blanket condemnations through the use of imprecise or misleading epithets.

4. The menace of 'indoctrination'

On the whole, the discussions about the place of religion in schools in recent decades have been carried on in an atmosphere of tolerance and understanding, even where there has been a clear clash of views or a conflict of interests. Of recent years, however, some of the opposition to religious education in our maintained schools has become more strident and less reasoned. It is significant that together with this change in tone, the discussion has tended increasingly to use a highly emotive and highly imprecise term—'indoctrination'. It has become so popular that we feel it demands careful examination in order to discover what useful purpose —if any—it serves.

Since the term is used of instruction over the whole field of human learning, it will be helpful first to consider the word in a wider educational context. One of the most influential of modern philosophers to affect current educational ideas and methods has been the American, John Dewey. Much present practice in English as well as American schools, and the theory which underlies it, derive from views which he propounded.

All teachers, and especially progressives, are aware of the dangers of indoctrination. But we easily deceive ourselves, and this can be seen in no less a case than that of Dewey himself who, after denouncing indoctrination, goes on apparently to commend the practice, and finally accepts the name.

In one of his essays published in 1935 dealing with education and democracy he discussed academic freedom.[1] He pressed for a new social orientation of the teaching profession, a forward-looking outlook in line with the scientific, techno-logical and industrial forces of the present in the interest of the freedom, security and cultural development of the masses. The tendency of the whole school system of the 1930s in the U.S.A. Dewey believed to be backward-looking, characterised by undemocratic social consequences and the almost automatic maintenance of the privileges of a small class. Dewey acknow-ledged that his advocacy of the new scientific orientation was a 'belief'— his support of it suggests it has something of the nature of a 'cause' and is a decided committal—yet at the same time he believed that he had arrived at his position, not by a "process of inculcation" but by "an intelligent study of historical and existing forces and conditions" later called "the method of intelligence".[2] In this context he referred to the influence of the press in a capitalist economy, and found it not surprising that "the press should itself be a business enter-prise conducted for profit, and hence carry on a vast and steady *indoctrination* in behalf of the order of which the press is

[1] "The Teacher and his World" reprinted in John Dewey *Philosophy of Education* (Littlefield, Adams and Co., 1964), pp. 70–82.
[2] *ibid.*, p. 81.

a part.''[1] In his view the schools had one great task— ''to
develop immunity against the propaganda influence of press
and radio'', since these were ''two of the most powerful means
of inculcating mass prejudice''.[2] Hitler's Germany was cited
as the example of a community in which the schools failed to
''create a popular intelligence which is critically discriminating''. Dewey's remedy for this dangerous situation was ''an
intelligent understanding of social forces given by schools''.[3]

The whole of Dewey's discussion bristles with assumptions
and difficulties the more closely it is examined. Even if we
grant, with Dewey, that ultimately three forces control society
—habit, coercive and violent force, and action directed by
intelligence—it is not at all clear that all reactionaries *unintel-
ligently* resist change, or that radicals always appeal to the use
of force. Neither is it clear that the schools and the teaching
profession *must* have some social orientation in the over-
simplified way Dewey defines it. The choice is rarely between
whether we look to the past or whether we look to the future.
It is not surprising that when Dewey uses the word 'indoctrination' in this essay, it similarly lacks clear definition. It is
a bludgeon word to batter his opponents, particularly the
press, whose sole interest, he asserts, is to maintain the *status
quo* out of which they derive so much material profit,
and to discourage ''critical discrimination''. Opposed to
''indoctrination'' (undefined but clearly bad) is ''the method of
intelligence'' (also undefined but clearly good) which Dewey
himself advocates, and which he seems to assert as the monopoly
of those whose views are ''forward-looking'' and possess
critical discrimination. That the *status quo* could itself be
defended by intelligent or discriminating thinkers is not
admitted.

Three years later, in 1938, Dewey published an essay

[1] *loc. cit.*, our italics.
[2] *ibid.*, p. 82.
[3] *loc. cit.*

entitled "What is social study?"[1] In it he urged that we should find the unity of the curriculum in social studies. By this he did not mean that a narrow sociological or economic syllabus should be added as an option or an extra discipline to existing subjects, but rather that all subjects at present studied should be directly related to their social and cultural effects and possibilities. "The natural focus, the assembling point, of the various studies is their social origin and function."[2]

In the final paragraph of this essay Dewey seems cautiously to allow teaching to be equated with indoctrination when the aim of such teaching is preparation for a different social order. He actually refers to "what is called indoctrination, or, if one prefer, teaching."[3] He argues that there is a danger that social studies as a separate discipline will become "organs of indoctrination in the sense of propaganda for a special social end, accepted enthusiastically perhaps, but still dogmatically."[4] On the other hand, "young people who have been trained in all subjects to look for social bearings will also be educated to see the causes of present evils. They will be equipped from the sheer force of what they have learned to see new possibilities and the means of actualising them."[5] The confused optimism of these words makes pathetic reading today; it is hard to realise that they were written less than thirty years ago. We notice at once that to see the social bearings of a given situation by no means enables a young person to identify the causes of present evils. Indeed we must go further. The very identification of a present evil depends on the prior acceptance of some form of value system. No sheer force of facts, however thoroughly mastered, logically brings with it a conviction about the rightness or wrongness of anything.

The way Dewey concludes this second essay shows that he

[1] ibid., pp. 180–183.
[2] ibid., p. 183.
[3] loc. cit.
[4] loc. cit.
[5] loc. cit.

in fact desires children to learn more than facts, and more than the social consequences of certain courses of action. In the earlier essay we mentioned, the press was assumed to be an evil influence *both* because it tended to perpetuate the traditional social system *and* because it encouraged uncritical acceptance of the older social values. Both the end and the means were found wanting. Since these two reasons were given, it was not clear whether one or both of them were basic to Dewey's critique. Was it the values transmitted which made such 'indoctrination' repugnant, or was it the means or mode of transmission which was objectionable? The close of this second essay makes it clear which element is fundamental for Dewey. He is actually able to toy with the idea that progressive ideas, being right and good in some ultimate sense which he does not define, may be transmitted in *any* way provided the teaching is successful, in other words provided that the Deweyite value system is accepted in the end. It is for this reason that he is able to conclude with the highly significant words; "They (the young people) will be indoctrinated in its deeper sense without having had doctrines forced upon them."[1] There cannot be much doubt about his meaning here. Specific social studies present the student with definite dogmas for acceptance or rejection. But an all-pervasive Deweyite orientation of the whole syllabus avoids overt and conscious presentation of doctrines. The student is not challenged to accept or reject. He will have accepted the interpretation of life offered without even having been conscious that a choice was to be made. This conclusion is one from which we shrink in horror, but there appears to be no possibility of avoiding the conviction that this *is* what Dewey was getting at.

The background of thought which lies behind Dewey's ambivalent use of the term 'indoctrination' seems to be this. Indoctrination is a teaching process connected with propaganda

[1] *loc. cit.*

and a deliberate dulling of the critical faculties. But it is an effective way of teaching—indeed, the 'learners' show remarkably energetic and definite changes of behaviour. And Dewey's progressive army of the future needs these characteristics. So he must first blur the distinction between teaching and indoctrination. Then as long as he is sure that his ultimate purpose is right (the Deweyite orientation of society) he can adopt methods which might appear to be reprehensible by established canons. The main thing is that these methods are effective. Such methods avoid clashes of principles and doctrines by going below the conscious level. They are methods probably most accurately described as indoctrination. Granted, this term has normally carried a pejorative sense. Dewey will avoid the implication by qualifying it. Values and orientation go over in a disguised form and the children are "indoctrinated *in its deeper sense*". To the progressive educator all methods are open. The end justifies the means.

This discussion of Dewey's ideas has enabled us to consider the issues raised by indoctrination in general. Two approaches seem to be suggested as the avenues of indoctrination. One is by way of the content of teaching, the other by way of certain methods of teaching. Interestingly enough the same tension between indoctrination as defined by the subject matter and indoctrination as essentially a teaching procedure is found in a recent English symposium on aims in education.[1] John Wilson takes the former view while R. M. Hare stresses the purpose or aim of the educator, which will of course affect the method. Hare's case contained a refutation of Wilson's rather confused position, to which we can only refer the reader here.

Our own position in this matter is that indoctrination is essentially a word which applies to a *method*. It denotes an

[1] See *Aims in Education*, ed. T. H. B. Hollins, (Manchester U.P., 1964), especially pp. 24–70.

educative procedure which is in a special way (to be discussed below) inappropriate to the particular topic being taught. But the point at which indoctrination begins or ends is differently situated for each particular domain of human thought or study. Nor is it the same for an individual at the various stages of his development.

We need first to distinguish between the realm of fact and the realm of value and belief in human experience. This division runs right through human knowledge, and since education seeks to initiate the rising generation into the inherited knowledge of the past, it must take account of this distinction which has emerged. In mathematics the distinction is non-existent. In the physical sciences the distinction is comparatively unimportant (the clear and well-known separation of observations from the theories meant to explain patterns of events in the physical world rarely causes trouble) but it is of great importance and delicacy in the humanities. In history, literature, art and religion there is certainly much relevant factual material, but choices between systems of interpretation have to be made, and these choices are not based on fact alone. This is not to say that such choices are merely individual preferences, purely random or irrational, but simply to say that judgments in this realm are more complex and more deeply rooted in personal experience than in other fields. Indoctrination is a term which highlights a particular kind of inappropriateness in each of these fields.

What does the term 'indoctrination' suggest when applied to teaching method in the more factual areas of human knowledge? It cannot mean simply the presentation of material for acceptance by children without any choice being offered or doubt allowed, since in many subjects the groundwork is almost invariably covered by this kind of teaching without anyone dreaming of objecting. These are the areas of established facts. It would be a waste of time to *argue* for the acceptance of everything that is taught in mathematics, science or geography. Life is too short, and in any case so much is universally accepted. Furthermore, the very nature of the schoolchild's limited capacity and reasoning power renders such a suggestion impossible. Where there is agreement on facts, they may be taught on authority in the early stages of learning— the authority of the teacher or the textbook. To speak of "indoctrinating geography" or "propaganda for the truths of mathematics" is nonsense.

Now as pupils progress in these fields, they will come to understand the particular techniques appropriate to each discipline and to see how the scientist (for example) collects, arranges and evaluates his facts. If the teacher does not enable his children to do this, then in the end he may be indoctrinating. R. S. Peters prefers to call the earlier stage by a neutral term, 'instruction', since there is no alternative mode of education. Only when the child is capable of being equipped to probe, question and to use the tools and procedures developed by investigators in the particular subject, but is denied these opportunities, can we speak of indoctrination. The teacher who denies to his pupils the right to investigate his subject independently, but continues to spoon-feed them, may justly be said to be indoctrinating. There must be a relaxing of teacher control once the child has been adequately equipped to assess and criticise. As Peters says, the teacher "has to teach in such a way that his students can eventually dispense with him".[1] Our students are learning techniques of exploration as well as what past and present pioneers have discovered. The significance of indoctrination in these fields is thus fairly clear.

But what of the other more complex areas of human knowledge? Once we leave the purely factual and empirical field, the term 'indoctrination' acquires a new significance. This is not so much because the domains involving values and beliefs

---

[1] *op. cit.*, p. 201.

are non-factual areas of human experience, but rather because their full significance is only grasped by a process which involves insight and a more personal approach. Facts about Shakespeare, Leonardo, Socrates or Beethoven may be given and learned, but the acquisition of such knowledge does not constitute literary, artistic, moral or musical awareness. Such knowledge is not yet the kind of knowledge which the teacher hopes for. The factual techniques appropriate to the set types of knowledge are largely historical (the life and times of . . .,seeing men against their cultural background) and technical (concerned with the particular media and forms they employed and the state of the particular arts in which they excelled). These things we may and must teach. But the child's particular awareness of the beauty, greatness, penetration, or relevance to the human situation of a given man's achievement in one of these fields is not at the teacher's command. The teacher can only try to provide the right conditions for it to 'occur'.

It is no longer regarded as appropriate (if it ever was) to try to force children to love Mozart's music or the poetry of Milton. Statements about greatness and sublimity in the arts are not thereby emptied of all public or factual significance. What we are saying is that coming to *see* that this man is a greater writer than that one is a process of learning which we cannot produce at a particular juncture in the educational process. We study, discuss and analyse, but then we can only wait for the penny to drop. We give relevant facts, but these may not bring about the real appreciation we wish the child to experience and enjoy. As teachers we feel it part of our responsibility to the child and to the subject to prepare the ground as carefully as possible in the hope that real appreciation will come. Further than this we must not go. Hence we are content to leave the final effect to time, further experience and other influences. And to face the fact that it may never occur at all.

There is a further feature of these domains which needs to be noted here. There is not always universal agreement on the 'correct' judgments in the humanities. Not every character or work enjoys an agreed position on the scale of evaluation. In these conditions we would usually consider it right to introduce students to possible alternatives. We explain that sincere and sensitive men have differed in their evaluation at certain points, and where possible, try to show how and why they arrived at their different positions.

Indoctrination in these fields may now be defined more clearly. It may be on the one hand an attempt either to compel a spurious insight, or to induce an outward response which indicates an awareness but which does not reflect a genuine consciousness of personal evaluation. The regurgitation of second-hand judgments in literature or art criticism has always been rightly censured. Insight is unavoidably personal. On the other hand, indoctrination may also consist of the refusal to consider with students the genuine options where such exist. It is open to students to consider Beethoven crude and self-assertive and Rembrandt a man with one gimmick only. From the nature of true awareness in these fields, it follows that no-one can be forced to fall in with one particular opinion, whether of the majority or of the individual teacher. That there is a vast majority vote in one direction suggests that there is something there to be seen, but it compels no one to see it himself. We do violence to the awareness we are hoping to foster if we attempt to persuade or compel a pupil to repeat as his own either a majority or an individual opinion. This would be indoctrination. The same objection would be raised against the technique of presenting children with various views only when they are so conditioned that all but the teacher's opinions would be rejected.

Some would say that morals and religion are realms of human experience in which no consensus at all has emerged

over the centuries.[1] In morals, however, a case can be made for
the gradual approach to a consensus, both along the lines of
sheer self-interest and social expediency (this is basically the
Kantian position which R. S. Peters re-states) and along the
lines of a comparison of various moral systems widely separated
in space and time.[2] Hence, although moral values are only
worth-while when they are freely accepted by an individual,
there is a place for teaching about past moral leaders and
teachers, and the systems which they advocated. Just as musical
awareness comes through listening to music, so moral awareness comes, at least in part, through thinking about moral
principles and situations which call for moral responses and
decisions. In so far as morals are reducible to doctrines, indoctrination is clearly a possibility. It would consist in the attempt
to implant one system of behaviour in the minds of children
without giving them the opportunity for reasoned discussion
of alternatives and by simply using bare authority to justify
acceptance—"because I say so" or "because society demands
it". Where a society is agreed on a group of underlying moral
principles, it would seem reasonable that these should be
explained and stressed in the schools, but never to the ex-
clusion of all other views.[3] Genuine moral education which
avoids indoctrination will never eschew comparative study
and discussion. There may be questioning at any and every
point as long as the whole process is characterised by a serious,
rational approach and the importance of a personal involvement in these matters is made clear.

So far there is very little moral education as such specifically
provided for in the timetables of British schools. But religion
is there. In the light of the foregoing discussion the nature
of religious indoctrination now emerges. Religious indoctrina-

---

[1] Wilson is very pessimistic here, Hare considerably less so. See their essays
referred to earlier, especially pp. 27–30,and 59–63.

[2] See C. S. Lewis, *The Abolition of Man* (Bles, 1946).

[3] In fact we need a particular system to use as a concrete example. Hare explains
how this may be done without indoctrination, *op. cit.*, p.62.

tion would be on the one hand to compel a response to the religious message, to demand—or at least to aim deliberately for—a personal commitment by all pupils to the Christian faith. Or on the other hand it would be to teach the Christian faith as if it were the only religion, or that only knaves and fools were unbelievers.

As in the case of morals, there is clearly a bias in favour of the study (though not the acceptance) of one particular religion because it is so intimately linked with our own culture, and because the people of the land desire their children to know about this faith, rather than a broad syllabus of all faiths to be taught to their children.[1] But the stress cannot be on the acceptance of this belief, because such acceptance has the nature of insight, and cannot be compelled. All that can be compelled is a spurious conformity which no educator, Christian or secularist, would want in any field. We are all opposed to indoctrination. The emphasis must remain where it has usually been laid—on the factual side. Children need a basic knowledge of the contents of the Bible, of the kind of individual lives and social systems which have emerged from the acceptance of this faith, and of the structure of Christian doctrine and its relevance in the world today. Young people need to know about these matters before they can take an informed decision as to whether the matter is worth pursuing. It is this factual knowledge, principally consisting in historical accounts which forms the bedrock of religious teaching. In addition to this we may well try to show how it *feels* to be a believer and the particular problems which this has involved in various situations; this is a more 'poetic' approach, and the kind of methods appropriate here may well be similar to those used in helping children to understand poetry and music and novels. Such a sympathetic involvement will aim at getting inside the skin of the characters chosen for study, and their message.

[1] Even Wilson recognises the weakness of this latter course: *op. cit.*, p. 31.

Such a taxing teaching task falls far short of indoctrination. It leaves children free to make their own choice. But it puts them in a position to see religious faith as a matter of importance, and as a matter for informed decision. It cannot in any significant sense be called indoctrination.

It is our hope that this term will in future be used in a clearly defined sense in the continuing discussions about religious education. Our analysis of Dewey's use of the term has shown that progressive thinkers as well as others have failed on occasion to make clear the conceptual area covered by the term 'indoctrination'. The word can mask shifts of emphasis and even ideas alien to a truly liberal and rational educational method. Our examination of its significance suggests that it can be used to refer to a particular type of educational approach, but that the precise meaning of indoctrination in terms of methodology can only be established by examining both the particular topic and the teaching situation in which indoctrination is said to occur.

CHAPTER IV

Content and Method

THERE is plenty of lively argument about the content and methods of religious education today. Attacks come from both outside and inside the subject. From the outside a minority view such as that of the secular humanist may briefly be expressed as follows—that education is the purpose of the school and religion is the business of the Church. The Newsom Report, *Half Our Future*,[1] probably expresses a majority view in the chapter "Spiritual and Moral Development". Here the position is strongly expressed that the full education of the pupil is incomplete without the interpretation of life which religious education offers and the values by which he may live. He may reject both, but at least he should know so that he may decide for himself. However, the most serious attacks on present religious education have come from within the teaching profession itself, and these are our immediate concern.[2] During the past few years a number of surveys have been carried out to assess the results of religious education under the 1944 Act, by means of factual tests and personal interviews. Two of the most publicised of these were the tests carried out by a group of teachers working with the Institute of Education of Sheffield

---

[1] H.M.S.O., 1963.
[2] Some of these writers form an outspoken school of thought which has attracted undue attention in recent years. Their books tend to be one-sided both in theology and in psychology, as a glance at the following works will show: R. Ackland *We Teach Them Wrong* (Gollancz, 1963); E. Cox *Changing Aims in Religious Education* (Routledge and Kegan Paul, 1966). Their general outlook appears to be shared by H. Loukes and Dr. R. Goldman.

67

University[1] and the investigations described by Harold Loukes in his *Teenage Religion*.[2] The results of both showed that pupils appeared to retain very little of what they were taught in school religious knowledge lessons, especially where such lessons were their only contact with religious teaching. This is disturbing but it is possible to exaggerate the significance of these findings. David Ayerst has pointed out[3] that an enquiry carried out by J. W. Packer at Leeds in 1952 showed that the teaching of history in schools was no more effective than the religious instruction, particularly as regards the retention of material taught. Furthermore there is much in good religious instruction which is not assessable by the methods usually employed. Nevertheless the surveys have rightly called in question the whole content and methods of religious education in our schools particularly at the secondary stage. There are further questions implicit in their findings. For instance, who should teach religious knowledge? And who, in fact, are the religious knowledge teachers? What are the qualities and qualifications necessary for a religious knowledge teacher who would make his subject alive and meaningful especially to the older pupil? Loukes has some useful suggestions to offer in the closing chapters of *Teenage Religion* and in the early chapters of his more recent *New Ground in Christian Education*.[4] The main position of Loukes may be summarised thus: "that the authoritative transmission of a received tradition must give way to the open search for living truth; that the hope of 'making children Christians' must yield to a hope of opening young eyes to look for themselves."[5] This statement contains an important insight into the methods of religious education, but it does not contain

[1] *Religion in the Schools* (University of Sheffield Institute of Education, Nelson, 1961).
[2] S.C.M. Press, 1961.
[3] In *Religious Education* 1944–1984 ed. A. G. Wedderspoon (Allen and Unwin, 1966), p. 68.
[4] S.C.M. Press, 1965.
[5] *ibid.*, p. 175.

all the truth. Our own position is that while, especially with older pupils, lessons must proceed with full and free discussion and through personal search, there must also be essential guidance from written sources, particularly Scripture, and from the experience of the teacher, if the discussion is to be fruitful and purposive.

Perhaps the most significant research into the nature of religious education is that which has sought to understand the processes by which children learn and the kind of material which is within the comprehension of pupils as they pass through various stages of intellectual development. Of this research probably the most important project so far has been that undertaken by Dr. Ronald Goldman and described in his book *Religious Thinking from Childhood to Adolescence*.[1] It is not possible to summarise the book adequately in this chapter especially as some of its assumptions, procedures and conclusions are open to serious question.[2] Dr. Goldman seeks to show that the conclusions of Jean Piaget concerning the learning stages through which children pass are as valid in the field of religious thinking as any other.

There are two broad conclusions which may be emphasised for the purpose of our discussion. Firstly, following Piaget, Goldman argues that the religious thinking of the pupil passes through three main stages. The first is the stage of pre-operational intuitive thought and covers the early school years up to the mental ages of seven and eight. The second stage, from the mental ages of eight to thirteen, is described as concrete operational thinking. The third stage (which some secondary school pupils never reach) is that of formal abstract thinking.

The implications of this are important. In the first stage,

[1] Routledge and Kegan Paul, 1964.
[2] Detailed criticisms will be found in K. Howkins *Religious Thinking and Religious Education*, (Tyndale Press, 1966), and in the article by C. M. Fleming "*Research Evidence and Christian Education*", reprinted in *Learning for Living*, Vol. 6, No. 1, September 1966, pp. 10–12.

the teacher must always be aware that the very young child is responsive to atmosphere and will best develop his religious sense through the beauty of worship and through the stories of personal kindness and the goodness of God. The teacher's own attitudes are of vital importance, especially his attitude to the Bible from which he will carefully select the stories most suited to the children of tender years. In the second stage, Goldman believes that the child will probably accept literally everything he is told or reads. Deeper religious concepts will not be understood. For his tests, Goldman selected three well-known Bible stories—Moses at the burning bush, the crossing of the Red Sea and the temptations of Jesus. After the children had heard these stories told in shortened form in modern English, Goldman put various questions to them in an attempt to assess the level of understanding reached by each child. His results appeared to show that these stories were often grossly misunderstood by primary school children, most of whom were satisfied with wrong explanations which later, he maintains, would create barriers to religious belief. Only in the third stage (beyond the capacity of many children) is the pupil capable of that abstract thinking which enables him to grasp fundamental religious conceptions and to discuss them intelligently,

Must we therefore admit that the Bible is not a children's book? Yes, in the sense that it is certainly not childish; nor would one begin in the lowest form at chapter I of Genesis to read straight through it as though it were an ordinary primer. If, however, the question implies that the Bible should be excluded from the classroom, especially in the junior school, then the answer must be "No". What Goldman found can equally be interpreted as showing the need for more careful selection of Biblical material and for a more intelligent presentation in the classroom of what is chosen.

There is a broad conclusion which may be drawn from

Dr. Goldman's research. Religious knowledge demands, like any other subject, that the best teaching methods, the most modern audio-visual aids and the most up-to-date textbooks shall be used in its service. Dull, unimaginative and insensitive teaching by those not really qualified to teach can only produce those lamentable results which are so widely add so rightly deplored. The implications of the conclusion have been known to experienced religious knowledge teachers for a long time.

The popularisation of recent research has led to an almost unanimous demand that the content of religious education as defined in the Agreed Syllabuses should be revised drastically, and that its methods must be considerably modified. In any discussion of Agreed Syllabuses it is essential to keep a sense of proportion. To advocate the abolition of all existing Agreed Syllabuses is far too extreme and is simply not practicable. The Agreed Syllabus represents a major advance in religious education and it embodies an important measure of agreement between local education authorities, Anglican and free churches, and the teachers. It seeks to ensure that a certain body of biblical and extra-biblical material is taught in all the schools of the local authority, gives valuable guidance in the preparation of schemes of work, and serves both the specialist and non-specialist alike. In some cases it has certainly saved pupils from the whims and fancies of individual teachers. What has been gained during the last twenty years must not be lightly discarded.

There are, however, certain specific criticisms of existing syllabuses which require careful consideration. These are

(i) that they are too academic, and therefore irrelevant to the needs of modern pupils in all schools.

(ii) their almost exclusive biblical emphasis makes them peculiarly unsuited for primary schools and secondary modern schools.

(iii) they are unsound educationally because the material presented is unsuited to the pupils' various stages of development.

(iv) they are unsuited to the needs of the average non-specialist teacher.

There is force enough in these criticisms to compel considerable revision of existing syllabuses and the following suggestions are offered as a contribution to the present discussion.

(i) Existing Agreed Syllabuses must be retained as a basis for revision. Complete abolition in order to begin afresh would lead to uncertainty and possibly to chaos.

(ii) The new syllabus should be prepared in three parts— (a) for the primary school pupils, (b) for the less able secondary school pupils, and (c) for the ablest secondary school pupils.

(iii) Help should be given in the preparation of schemes of work suitable for different conditions in the schools.

(iv) Material should be selected in order to meet the needs, spiritual, moral and mental, of the pupils from five to eighteen years.

(v) Sections should be included on methods of presentation with lists of suggested textbooks, audio-visual aids and other helps to teachers.

Attempts to carry out the fourth suggestion will probably arouse the greatest controversy, and it is therefore necessary to consider this suggestion further. The issue may be crystallised in the following question "What is the place of the Bible (and especially the Old Testament) in religious education today?" Some researchers would seem to imply that the Old Testament has very little importance at *any* stage, and almost none at the primary level. The New Testament too has been attacked on the grounds that much of it is beyond both the experience and the mental grasp of most pupils.

These contentions must be strongly challenged and their implications resisted. It is true that some Old Testament material would be better omitted from the primary school syllabus. Probably more use could be made of selections from the Psalms and from the Prophets—presented in a context of worship, of music and of art. This would certainly encourage and not hinder the religious development of younger children. Stories of Jesus are indispensable and should be carefully chosen without duplication.

In the first three years of the secondary course a solid foundation of biblical knowledge should be laid. Two years of this should be given to the New Testament, and one to the Old. One year should be devoted to a careful study of the life and teaching of Jesus and one to the rise and growth of the Early Church as recounted in Acts and relevant parts of the Epistles. In the year's study of the Old Testament particular reference should be made to the biography of its great men, especially the prophets, and so to God's revelation of himself to men culminating in the coming of Christ.

The fourth and fifth years in the secondary school might well be devoted to the contemporary Church in the world and to the study of personal, social and national problems which are important to young people today. Here again the Bible will have proper place as giving guidance and bringing illumination to discussion. Without doubt much more research is needed into the vital question of the suitability of biblical material at various stages of the pupil's school life, but what is offered above could be the basis of a workable scheme. It does not conflict with the assured results of any of the work that has already been done.

The other main implication of modern research into religious education is that methods and techniques need to be rethought in order to make the subject lively and relevant to pupils today. Methods in use during the past few years vary so much

from school to school that it is difficult to generalise. Certainly
dull, stereotyped teaching results in the failure which it
deserves. The experienced, well qualified teacher, however,
has been aware that he needs all the modern techniques in
the fields of audio-visual aids, dramatisation, art, music and
good textbooks that he can possibly acquire. The first requirement is that the teacher must be a skilled practitioner in the
art of using the Bible as the basic source of religious education.
Teaching the scriptures by an unvarying 'chalk and talk'
method is stultifying and is to be condemned. This is not to
deny that both chalk and talk have their rightful place in the
religious knowledge lesson, provided that the talk is a two-
way process of dialogue and that the teacher is skilled in the
use of the chalk. Furthermore there are many ways of using
the Bible and it is to be hoped that 'round the class' reading
verse by verse is no longer in use. Reading the Bible as a
preparation for study is a serious matter and should not be
attempted impromptu by pupils. The teacher himself should
set an example by his own reading, and full use should be made
of the various versions, with which he should be familiar.
Dramatised readings are effective where appropriate and the
choral reading of psalms and passages of poetic beauty might
well be assiduously practised. For more backward pupils with
limited vocabulary the versions provided by A. T. Dale[1] will
be found useful.

Above all, the teacher could well be guided by the early
Christians whom we find in Acts "searching the Scriptures".
Programmed learning is a modern technique, but the principle
is old enough. Many of the new textbooks employ the 'search'
technique, notably those produced under the general editor-
ship of Dr. Goldman.[2] The teacher should be aware of these
and consider whether such books meet his particular need.

[1] See the "New World" Series, (O.U.P., 1966).
[2] Published by Rupert Hart-Davis.

B. H. Smythe has also produced a series of "Search Books"[1] on programmed learning lines. Their content is more strictly biblical. His books are directed towards the more backward pupils in the lower forms of secondary schools. The teacher, however, need not be deterred by the absence of textbooks; he can prepare his own programmes of search, provided he knows the Bible and any other relevant textbooks available in the school. The important thing is to stimulate pupils to discover truth for themselves.

From this process of study should proceed informed discussion. The popular phrase here is 'the open-ended approach', and it is important to understand what this should mean. It should not mean what Professor D.E. Nineham, at a conference in 1965 called "the exchange of mutual mystification", the inevitable result of uninhibited discussion by pupils who are still ill-informed and lacking in experience.[2] Furthermore, while some children enjoy this, most are too well aware that they learn very little in such lessons. It should mean, however, a willingness to discuss freely and frankly in order to pursue the search for truth that has already begun in careful study of the text whether scriptural or non-scriptural. The story of the boy Jesus in the Temple provides us with the biblical model of what this should mean. It is impossible to exclude some degree of authority in the conduct of such lessons. But no competent teacher will take refuge in the answer "It is in the Bible", in order to exclude further discussion; on the contrary, the fact that "it is in the Bible" should mean that it is worthy of very careful consideration and intelligent discussion.

It is considered also that the fundamental technique of careful study and informed discussion will avoid the weakness of irrelevance which is a common criticism of much religious

---

[1] Published by Darton, Longman and Todd.
[2] *Religious Education* 1944–1984, p. 144.

knowledge teaching today. Relevance is not a moralising post-script tacked on to the end of a lesson; that subject is relevant which is felt by pupils to involve *them*, because issues are raised with which they are concerned. The Old Testament is not presented as a study in Jewish antiquities; those passages are selected, particularly from the prophets, which raise the 'issues of life' in every age—justice and oppression, sin and redemption, selfishness and compassion. The art of good religious knowledge teaching is to present these issues arrestingly and the biblical characters who raise them as our living contemporaries.

The importance attached to the Bible as our fundamental religious knowledge textbook does not exclude concern for the child. The selection of material and its presentation must *begin* within the abilities and the experience of the pupils, but it does not and cannot stay there. The "child-centred approach" is sometimes understood as teaching which is always within the understanding and experience of the child. This would be mistaken policy. As in any other subject, there must be a careful leading on from the known into the unknown, and in religious education this guidance and direction carries a great responsibility, for the pupil may not only come to know what he knew not, but he may also become what he was not. We would conclude, therefore, that good religious education should be child-centred and Bible-centred, and above all, Christ-centred.

All this presents a tremendous challenge to the religious knowledge teacher, and it is good that in recent years more aids have become available to help him. In the field of visual aids there are very valuable films and filmstrips to illustrate most themes within the subject. It is important to realise that they are only adjuncts to the lesson and not substitutes for it. Films are for occasional and especially revisional use; film strips should be used only in part, usually using not more than half a dozen frames at a time. They call for a suitably equipped classroom and some skill in the use of equipment. Charts, maps, and diagrams illustrating various themes may be bought, but the best can still be made by the teacher himself, building them up in the classroom and avoiding undue complexity. Inevitably this means that the teacher must seek to acquire the necessary skill, but the results make the trouble worthwhile. In the field of audio aids the teacher will find in the portable tape recorder a very great ally. The building up of a library of tapes takes time but the effort is rewarding. A lively school is an excellent source of material for the tape recorder. Dramatisation can illuminate a subject and recordings of such dramatic activity might well be stored on tape for future use. The school choir can also provide the alert religious knowledge teacher with recordings which can be profitably used. In all this the teacher is seeking variety of approach and presentation. There is simply no excuse for the dull, stereotyped lesson which conforms to one pattern. Religious education should be lively and exciting so that the pupils are conscious of doing something worthwhile. When it is so presented, motivation is unlikely to be wrong.

There is a further aspect to this question. Religious education can only be relevant to the pupil in so far as it is meaningful to him and is seen to have purpose in his own life and in the life of the school. This means that there must be more to religious education than the actual lessons in the classroom and the daily act of worship. An active Christian group in the school is an indispensable adjunct, because it brings religion into a wider context of worship and of community activity. "Inasmuch as ye did it to the least of these" is still one of the acid tests, and to guide a school fellowship into useful spheres of service is a most rewarding part of the religious knowledge teacher's task. Local community service is a valuable expression of this and is very worthwhile to senior pupils, whilst humanitarian work for the lepers, the orphans, all people in dire need in any part of the world, can be the work of the whole school.

In all this, one thing is essential and that is the quality of the teacher himself. In so far as the results of the 1944 Act have seemed to be disappointing, the main reason must be found here. That the position has improved is gratifying, but that there is much yet to be done cannot be denied. For the fully qualified and committed teacher there is a wonderful opportunity. There will be for him many disappointments, but the task is abundantly worthwhile.

CHAPTER V

The Lion's Den

MANY of those who speak and write about religious education have no recent experience of the classroom. The general public who are interested in the whole question have only the memories of their own schooldays to go upon. An accurate idea of what is involved in the confrontation between teacher and class is vital if we are to discuss constructively the present state of scripture teaching. So in this chapter we hope to show how far the classroom is still a lion's den, at any rate for the Daniels who teach religious knowledge.

An interested enquirer into the present state of theory and practice in religious education finds it difficult to gain a precise impression of any central body of thought or opinion. In this country things tend to develop without an overall pattern or standard works of reference. Many people, especially parents and those considering teaching as a profession, are curious to know what really goes on in the classroom. They want to know how scripture is being taught at a time when there seems to be much indifference and hostility to the Bible. What are the main problems peculiar to the subject? Is success possible? Above all, is it all worthwhile?

It is not our purpose to attempt an answer to all these questions, but rather to try to give some idea of what actually happens in the teaching of religious knowledge. Relatively few writers have attempted this, although in two of his books Harold Loukes has given his impressions of how some children react to the religious education they receive.[1] For this chapter a number of religious knowledge teachers in all types of state school were asked to tell something of their personal experiences in school, and what follows here is largely made up of their replies. From these incidents we may learn something of their work. By highlighting a few reactions, successes and failures from the experience of these teachers in the daily round of their life in school, it is possible to convey something of the 'feel' of the classroom.

At the outset it must be stressed that many people regard the task of the teacher through rose-coloured spectacles. One teacher with experience of mixed grammar and comprehensive schools in industrial Yorkshire stresses the ceaseless strain to which the religious knowledge teacher is exposed. There are many factors which combine to create this strain. The first is the difficulty of constantly changing classes. The room is never filled with the same faces from the start to the finish of the week. Hence one has to make a continual effort to remember names, the trouble-makers, the garrulous, the shy, the puzzled, and the atmosphere and problems of last week's lesson. Then there is the burden of having to give the same lesson four times over, assuming one is a scripture specialist without assistant staff in a four stream school. Again, the time one spends with each class is so short, and therefore so precious, that only meticulous preparation of every lesson will satisfy the conscientious teacher. Yet the opportunity is so great that a further temptation arises. The sincere and enthusiastic teacher will tend to want to spend each lesson on his feet—reading, explaining, asking and answering questions —so that at the end of the day he is in a state of physical and mental exhaustion.

A further important element has not yet been mentioned. The attitude of most children of secondary school age to

[1] *Teenage Religion* and *New Ground in Christian Education*.

religious knowledge teaching is different from their attitude to any other subject. In other lessons the child simply asks for the knowledge he has not got, and bows to the superior knowledge of the mathematics or history teacher. He willingly accepts the answer he is given. In the scripture lesson things are different. In the home an attitude of tolerant agnosticism towards religious truth has often been absorbed, and the earnest Christian teacher is accused of being dogmatic as he attempts to explain the Christian revelation. It does not come naturally to most children to acknowledge any authority in religious matters. Except in the rare cases where there is a living faith in the home, or where real understanding has been imparted through a good Sunday school, the teacher can assume no basic knowledge and no agreed procedure for progressing towards deeper religious understanding. As a result the attitude of an average class is often one which has to be resisted and changed before real learning can take place. It is this which contributes largely to the unique strain which is felt by the teacher.

The majority of religious knowledge teachers are convinced that the work they are doing is worthwhile. It is a challenging, responsible task. All teachers, whatever their subject, experience irritations and disappointments but scripture teaching in particular can be very frustrating as we have shown. Yet the importance of religious knowledge with its concern with the moral development of children and with the possibility of awakening awareness of the religious dimension of experience makes the subject crucial in the education of the young. As one modern school teacher wrote: "It has its ups and downs, and one needs to be very patient, but it makes the most vital contribution of all to the children's education. It's a real privilege to teach R.K." Today nearly all older children need to be convinced that the subject is worth studying. They want to know why they must learn religious

6

knowledge as well as all the other subjects. Loukes showed conclusively that children do not want to "do away with R.I.", but in the last two years of school there are many who only wish to learn the things which they think will help them in their future jobs. So comes the blunt question about scripture—"What good is it?"

One secondary modern school teacher of boys answered this by using the then current news of the great mail train robbery:

> In comparing R.I. with other subjects we discussed the robbery and decided that the train robbers were fit men (Physical Education), they knew the best place to go to (Geography), they knew all about timetables and the value of money (Mathematics), but somehow all this fitness and knowledge had only been used to harm others. Why? The boys quickly realised that character is important too, that here is where the Ten Commandments and the teachings of Jesus are most relevant, and that to live according to this teaching is essential.

Another schoolmaster meets most hostility from sixth formers. Apart from the two boys who, when asked by the headmaster to do some extra work, pointed out that they had only one free period available—they meant the scripture period—he says that many sixth formers object to religious knowledge lessons because they feel that it is a form of indoctrination. It is difficult, he adds, to persuade them that their increasing antipathy in fact shows that *they* are conditioned against Christianity.

Showing the relevance of biblical teaching to life in the second half of the twentieth century is an important part of the religious knowledge teacher's work. It is often harder to do this with Old Testament material, according to some teachers. But success comes in most unexpected ways, as one grammar school master working in south-east England indicates:

> Last year, the homework for a certain form was to read about King Saul and the Amalekites, and his disobedience. It happened that I had recently told several girls that they were not allowed to write on the blackboard. At the next R.I. lesson I arrived to find more writing on the board— remarks like "We love sir." So I rebuked them for their repeated disobedience and mildly punished those responsible. One girl complained that they had done it with the best of intentions, but on being questioned, admitted that it was sheer disobedience. Then I asked her what her homework was about. She began to tell me. Why did Saul keep some of the cattle? For sacrifice. Was that a good thing to do? Yes. Did God want sacrifice? Yes. So was Saul's motive good? Yes. Then why do you think that Samuel, God's prophet, was so angry with Saul? Because God had told Saul to kill all the animals. Right. Now was Saul's intention good? Yes. But was he sinning? Yes. There followed a long pause. Then a knowing smile crept over the girl's face. Do you see? Yes, sir...
>
> This happened last year. I mentioned it to her only a few days ago and she still remembers it.

One teacher taking a non-selective class of twelve- to thirteen-year-olds gave a lesson on the parable of the Good Samaritan. "Please, sir, I know what Samaritans were. It was a name for people who were kind to other people." After the parable had made its point, one child pointed out: "But, sir, if you help people like that, you *get put upon*." As the teacher comments: one successful lesson at least. Another example, linked with the same parable, comes from a primary school head teacher. He writes:

A black-browed, scowling Bryan was brought to me, together with a weepy-eyed little half-caste boy called Freddy. I had an apartheid problem on my hands. The reason Bryan gave was short and to the point. "I don't like niggers. My dad says they killed his uncle. So I bashed him." He did not seem to be in the right mood for a heart-to-heart at that moment and my angry disapproval made no apparent impression. But God works in a mysterious way. It was after a simple talk in which the good Samaritan figured that a shamefaced Bryan came to me and with the simplicity that only children can employ, he told me he was sorry. He and Freddy became the best of friends — but oh what damage adults can do!

It is easy to be too dogmatic about what material is suitable or unsuitable for particular age groups. Research on this is only in its infancy and much more is needed. However, children often surprise their teachers with illuminating comments. A northern grammar school master illustrates this and at the same time makes a vital acknowledgment too often overlooked or ignored by some who comment on religious education today.

As I reflect upon twenty years' experience as a religious instruction specialist in the classroom, I am conscious that the Holy Spirit does guide both teacher and taught, and that the younger pupil may well illustrate the truth of Scripture that out of the mouths of babes and sucklings praise has been perfected. One of the most difficult lessons to teach concerns the experience of Jesus on the mount of Transfiguration. No adult would claim to understand all that this meant to Christ. With ID, almost at the end of their first year, I had read the passage quietly after the necessary introduction, and then we pursued our inquiry into what this could mean. One pupil shyly volunteered his suggestion—that "heaven and earth seem to meet on the mountain with Jesus". He was not altogether sure what he meant by this but nonetheless he was expressing what for him was a real God-given intuition. The class was very interested, and the discussion which followed was very well worthwhile for all of us.

As this master goes on to say, "the comprehension of religious truth often lies beyond the pupil's ability to express coherently and logically, but this is also true at times of the teacher."

A teacher in the north-east supplies another example:

I was taking a class of backward 14–15 year olds (most could not read or write) and was trying to deal with the message of Isaiah chapter vi. The word 'holy' got no response, so I turned to the usages of the word, e.g. Holy Bible, and tried to get some sort of answer to its meaning. Kenneth put up his hand and said, "It's like my sock, sir." I had fallen for that type of answer before so I nipped in the bud such a suggestion. To my annoyance he persisted in saying that the meaning of 'holy' was like his sock. Finally, I asked him to illustrate his answer on the blackboard and he was so serious about the matter that he immediately left his seat, took the chalk, drew the warp and weft and then with a wetted finger made the hole. I still disagreed with him and repeatedly pointed out the difference between 'hole' and 'holy'. In exasperation he said, "Sir, I am sorry but you cannot see it", and drawing a line to represent one strand he drew his finger across to represent a small break. "You see, sir, when a little stone gets into your shoe it cuts the wool but it does not stay cut but springs apart. God and us have been joined together, something has come between and cut the strand, we have sunk lower and God's end has gone higher." I saw it and

it has been my illustration ever since—sin cuts, sin sepa-
rates and we are cut off from the higher quality of life
which God ordained for us.

Another grammar school master from the south recalls "many
very valuable discussions arising on not making idols" in a
series of lessons on the Ten Commandments. With second
forms, the sort of reply he has received is "We do not know
what God looks like", and "God has not got a body". He
continues:

> Pursuing this further we find that it does not make sense
> to think of God with a body, as He could then be in only
> one place at once, and would not be all-powerful. Here
> I have spent a whole period discussing the nature of God—
> with a second form! One boy remarked that God could not
> have a body because He existed before atoms. A good
> point. Gradually we get over the idea of God as Spirit.

From this can follow discussions on prayer and on the idea
of God as a Person.

> Children usually think this means that God has a body and
> so they object to the term. So we argue that a person has a
> body, but the real person is the character, and so when we
> say we know a person we mean, not that we recognise his
> body, but that we know him, his character. In this sense
> God is a Person, like us, but not limited as we are.

A most remarkable incident is related by a young teacher of a
reception class in Birmingham, and her story illustrates how
the mind of a child sometimes works in strange, unpredictable
ways. She had been taking lessons on flowers, trees, grass,
with the aim of bringing out beauty, and she asked the class to
illustrate by drawings. One showed flowers, trees and sun,
but marked all over the drawing were Crosses. When asked

why the drawing had been so disfigured the girl replied, "Miss, you can't see, but behind what I see is God."

Teaching about the Holy Spirit is always difficult. One delightful story from a secondary modern school master who had been reading the Nicodemus story with his second form tells how one boy, a Sunday school superintendent's son, stayed behind after the lesson.

> He said he liked the lesson but could I prove the part about the Holy Spirit. I told him that Jesus said He would send the Holy Spirit to those who believe. Jesus always spoke the truth, and as I believe in Him and have asked for the gift, He lives in me. "But how do you *know*?" asked the boy. I replied that whenever I am asked a difficult question, I ask for God's Holy Spirit to speak through me. The boy looked at me and replied: "He does too. You never lose, do you?"

Prayer is a subject in which many children are interested, particularly the younger ones. This is especially the case if it is seen to be a reality in the life of the teacher himself. One London primary school headmaster sometimes asks the children for suggestions for prayer in school assembly. Such opportunies may, however, have surprising results.

> One Friday some years ago a ten-year-old shot up his hand and asked with a great deal of fervour that I should pray that Millwall should not be relegated to the Fourth Division. I detected a certain feeling of sympathy from the amused teachers round the borders of the Hall and stumbled through an answer that I would pray for all sportsmen. Later I had a chat with John and he seemed to be satisfied with my explanation that sportsmanship and playing the game were the things we should pray for. Sad to relate, John's favourite team went down. However, some time

later John's sister Jeanne came to meet me one morning with a wide grin. "John's prayers have been answered, sir. They've gone up again."

A grammar school master says he finds the stories of Jacob well received by first forms who seem to understand Jacob's character as a cheat, and how he first had a personal experience of God at Bethel, after previously having just heard about God.

> Then we see from the way Jacob prayed to God, almost trying to cheat Him, and the fact that God did not seem to mind, that God really wanted Jacob, not because he *was* a good fellow, but to make him one. It was a 'bad' prayer but at least he prayed, and that pleased God. Discussion follows on prayer, and learning this by trying. This goes down well.

With this interest in prayer goes an almost equal interest in the fact that God speaks to men. Children are especially intrigued and concerned that He speaks to particular individuals. The story of Elijah and the still, small voice provided one opportunity to discuss this subject. "He never talks to me, sir," challenges one child. "Are you sure?" "Yes, sir." "Have you ever listened to try to hear Him?" "No, sir." The teacher observes that it is important for many children to realise that they have never given God a chance to speak to them and that they must take care and listen properly—ways of doing this are discussed—if they would hear Him. Nonetheless one north-country teacher in a rural grammar school met a pupil four years after the boy had left school at sixteen, and was asked: "Do you remember telling us that God spoke to us? Well, I'm still waiting."

Many and varied are the questions that children sometimes ask. One comprehensive school teacher remarked that the difficult questions she has been asked are usually of the non-sense type, such as "Who made God?" All religious knowledge teachers have their share of these. But some pose a real problem for the questioner, like the fourth form boy who demanded: "Please, sir, if God hates war, why do ministers of religion hold a service on board a nuclear submarine when it's launched?" Or the third form grammar school girl who asked: "Sir, good people who trust God go to heaven when they die, don't they?" "Yes." "And they're happy there, aren't they?" "Yes." "Then why did Jesus bring back Lazarus?" Or again, the fourth-year leaver in a non-selective form, two weeks before the end of the term, who, as the teacher went round the class to see the way an assignment was being tackled, wanted to know: "Is God angry with people who don't believe in Him? I've thought about it a lot, and I can't quite believe. Is He angry with me?"

Discipline is often more of a problem at first for the religious knowledge teacher than for his or her colleagues. This is due firstly to the fact that many pupils display sceptical indifference to the subject, which is a fashionable attitude. Secondly, many classes have only one period per week of religious instruction. As many teachers point out, to be known in connections other than scripture lessons is often a great help in establishing understanding and friendliness. As well as the school Christian group meeting after school, outings to the baths or ice-rink, sports functions, and educational visits during half-term breaks (to use one modern school teacher's examples) "all give the pupils a chance to see the R.I. teacher as a human being whose good points they appreciate and whose weaknesses they tolerate with Christian charity—'Old so-and-so is not so bad'." Friendliness and firmness go together. One south Yorkshire grammar school master says:

In my second year of teaching, with 5B with whom the year
before I had had disciplinary problems, I was asked: 'Sir,
you reckon that you're a very good Christian?'' ''No . . .
I'm a Christian but not a very good one.'' ''Sir, you're a
Christian. Why then did you keep us in last year?'' ''M'Kin-
lay, if I'd been a better Christian I'd have kept you in
much longer.'' A valuable discussion of first principles
followed.

There is a piquant touch from one teacher in whose first
lesson with fourth form grammar school girls some pupils
tried to test the teacher, and were quickly disciplined. Later
in the lesson a note was intercepted which read: ''You'd
think God would have sent us somebody *kind* to teach R.I.''
Likewise in a first lesson, again with girls but this time fourth
form B and C stream pupils in a secondary modern school,
such early reactions were heard as ''I think he's queer.'' ''He
doesn't *look* queer.'' ''We sent the last one up the wall after
three weeks.'' Problems of discipline are more common, for
all teachers at the secondary stage, with middle school
children. One modern school master of wide experience
remarks that towards the end of the third year some boys
make their own personal response to the Christian faith.
''Others who have attended Sunday school and church clubs
renounce their beliefs and will idle and sulk if allowed. They
need friendship and understanding, especially those 'C'
stream tough guys who put on such an air of strength and
confidence and are at heart deeply afraid. It is the older forms
who are ready to discuss, and to deride.''
Discussion lessons are most popular with the older pupils,
and some teachers base their lesson content on whatever subjects come up from their classes. The stock problems of
science and religion are commonly raised in most fifth and
sixth forms. Among these, outdated 'contradictions' crop up

regularly. For instance, many children think that Darwinian evolution satisfactorily explains everything about man, not merely our biological history; also that Christians still believe that world history began in the year 4004 B.C. Far too many pupils think that the approach and methods of science are the only possible and valid ones whatever the subject being studied. More than one scripture specialist has had cause to wish that some of his colleagues were more up-to-date, or encouraged a more tentative approach to complex problems especially in science.[1] Particularly popular topics for discussion are 'proofs' for the existence of God, which are usually debated eagerly. One grammar school master gives a regular series of lessons on the evidence for the resurrection based on Professor J. N. D. Anderson's booklet.[2] Among reactions he has received is a frequent one that "it seems convincing but they do not feel there is a God". In other words, "they feel that it sounds reasonable, and seems proved, but they have no personal experience. From here we discuss sin as a barrier. And so on." A grammar school mistress once took a term's course with a fifth form beginning with discussion on "What is a Christian?" and ranging over topics chosen by the class. A written and anonymous assessment at the end of the course included one comment that the writer had learned more from the lessons than from all her confirmation classes. On the other hand another grammar school master points out that "in discussion it is always easier for the cynic to speak rather than the idealist, the unbeliever rather than the seeker or believer. This puts a wrong emphasis on the discussion." A not uncommon experience is that of the eager teacher who, having expounded his theme, hopes to set off discussion and cheerfully asks for "Any questions?"

[1] This is not to suggest that R. K. teachers are never over-dogmatic or out-of-date. For example, many of the theories of Form and Higher Criticism which once held sway but which now have been rejected or considerably modified by recent research, are still being taught at classroom level.

[2] Published by I.V.F.

Up goes a hand. "Please, sir, it's time for my dental appointment."

Discussions on issues of sex and morality are especially common with fourth and fifth forms in all types of secondary school. These often prove personally very challenging to individual members of the class. One master in a technical school teaching a lesson on honesty to fifteen-year-old boys was suddenly challenged. The lesson's theme was that we do not really ever get away with dishonesty, but one boy vehemently asserted that we do. After several minutes the master, sensing that something was greatly concerning this boy, asked him to illustrate his argument. He confessed that he had once not paid his bus fare and had never been detected. Further questioning revealed that this had happened over six years earlier. The boy was still acutely ashamed.

An equally unexpected personal problem came up after a "sex-education-cum-R.E.-lesson" to the first year sixth form in a comprehensive school, when one girl privately informed the mistress that no one had ever told her that a baby was nine months in the womb before birth. She now knew that her parents were unmarried when she was conceived. She then asked: "Do you think that's why they're always having rows? They don't respect each other."

Most of the experiences recounted for this chapter are, like the one just recorded, concerned with individual pupils. This is not surprising since in the end teaching is a matter of personal relationships between individuals, and the more memorable incidents are usually connected with particular pupils. Perhaps the taste of the scripture classroom may best be savoured through sharing some of these actual experiences of practising teachers.

There was the comprehensive school agnostic who took religious knowledge at 'O' level, then went on to study it for 'A' level, and who told the teacher, "Well, I'm glad we did the fourth gospel. It makes better sense of Christianity than anything else I've read.'' A grammar school master tells of a sensitive upper sixth former for whom it was agony to hear the master, at the request of the class, explain the Book of Revelation as he understood it.

> The boy did not know whether to argue all the time or not at all. I quietly suggested to him that for the next week or two he should makes notes on what *I* said. Then *he* could say how he understood the book. He agreed, and I helped him in making his interpretation clear. His hearers were convinced he was wrong, but he felt he had been fairly treated.

A senior mistress in another comprehensive school remembers the nineteen-year-old just off to college who confessed that she had always been scared of death, funerals and coffins, and had never told anyone of her fears until that moment. Now after having worked through 'O' and 'A' levels in religious knowledge (the teacher always urging them to question and bring up problems) she had lost that fear. Now she could think of death or see a funeral without panic. There was the four-teen-year-old schoolboy who claimed to have religious scruples about homework, whenever he got behind with it, only to be told by his wise religious knowledge teacher that he could indeed develop his scruples—when he'd caught up with his work. After this, the boy's mother came to the school to defend and plead for her son and to complain about the atti-tude of the scripture master. Poor lad. The headmaster was just as adamant, and the boy had to do his homework. Again. there was a very moving radio account of the Easter story, listened to with close attention by the seven- to eight-year-old class in a Bedfordshire primary school. In the silence which followed, the voice of one child suddenly burst out, "Is it true?" The rest of the class immediately assured him that it was.

Most teachers feel that much of their work seems to be lacking in real achievement, with little that is tangible to show for all their conscientious work. Only one, fortunately, wrote of the comprehensive school girl who threatened her with a razor blade. A primary school teacher sums up for the majority:

> Time and again I tell myself that it is all a waste of time, that I am beating my head against a brick wall. As I grind out the same of kind thing I wonder how much is going in.

Nevertheless many teachers admit with pleasure that many children come to thank them when they leave school. It is only then that some will shyly confess that they read their Bible every day and pray regularly. Success *is* enjoyed, and often unexpectedly. One secondary school master was encouraged when one pupil privately told him: "Some of the boys think you are too dogmatic" and "They also think you are too sympathetic to the outlook of the unbeliever". This same teacher was once told by his headmaster that one mother had sent her son to their school "because of what the scripture master stood for". Another grammar school master learned of a fifth former who started to attend church, in due time was confirmed, and was now a keen church member. This change began as a result of a class discussion, but it was not until long afterwards that the master was told of this outcome of his teaching. Similarly a secondary modern school master mentions a boy now training to be a religious knowledge teacher. "I hardly noticed him in school," he says, "but the boy says he remembered my teaching." A primary school teacher relates how a mother told him that her daughter, when aged only six, had been much impressed by his illustration about the policeman and how he holds our hand to help us. "You said she could put her hand into the hand of Jesus when she returned to her classroom—and she did. It was as simple as that." Lastly there is the devastating story that one master tells. After expounding a particularly difficult passage, he asked an all-important question, to decide whether the real meaning had been grasped by the class or not.

I had just come to the conclusion, after an uncomfortably long pause, that I had been wasting my time and that I should have to start all over again, when one girl put up her hand. This is it at last, I thought triumphantly. "Yes, Mary," I said with an encouraging smile. And back came the answer, "Please, sir, your underpants are showing."

There are other sparks from the grindstone too. After a lesson on John the Baptist and his fiery message, followed up by the class having to draw their impressions of the story, one young child portrayed a fierce-featured, black-bearded figure exhorting, "Repent ye fatheads". Another primary school girl had drawn a number of what appeared to be footprints in her picture of Moses at the burning bush. When asked what these marks were she earnestly replied, "They are the holes. Like you said, Moses was standing on holy ground. " Answers to second form grammar school examination papers included Paul being scoured in the barracks, Peter denying Jesus three times before the cockroaches, and Jesus saying that you should not have two or three or four husbands unless you were properly divorced. And there was a superb answer from one primary school boy to the test question: Who are the three Persons of the Trinity? He wrote, with complete confidence, "Mr. Wood, Mr. Sheppard and Mr. Potter" (the vicar and his two curates).

A number of revealing glimpses emerge from most of the stories related in this chapter about the nature and needs of children. We see something of their behaviour, their difficulties, their charm and their frankness, and thus of the attractiveness and fascination of teaching them. In this task there are two chief problems which most teachers acknowledge. As one primary school headmistress says, one must try firstly to teach without preaching, and secondly to make it clear to children that Jesus lives still and that God cares for them individually. Concerning the second she adds: "Perhaps this can only be learned through the character of the teacher who is known by the children both to care and to be trusted." This last point, as most teachers testify, is crucial. Another sums up thus: "So I feel that teaching the Gospel in schools involves not only imparting knowledge by a teacher but the way of life of each individual, whether child, class teacher or head." Conditions vary from school to school but even the worst have unexpected advantages, as a primary school headmistress from Middlesbrough indicates:

> The very old school in which I teach is too compact, with a very small yard shared with the Infants' school, so we are severely lacking in space. The immediate neighbourhood is very congested, having narrow streets of terraced houses without gardens at all. These adverse conditions, incongruously, give fertile ground for communication of the Gospel, because children and adults must, of necessity, learn to share and to consider the safety and welfare of others.

All would agree with the view of one schoolmaster who has taught in both old and cramped, and spaciously modern surroundings that what really matters is not conditions but relationships.

All that has been said in this chapter indicates that in the schools the challenge of religious knowledge can be met with wisdom, sympathy and skill. Certainly the very best is demanded of a fully trained teacher and the disappointments almost invariably outweigh the encouragements. Only rarely can the zealous amateur fully succeed and there is no place for the unwilling 'volunteer'. What is it really like to be a teacher of scripture? The last word should come from a specialist of long experience. "Church people, particularly clergymen, are always reminding me of the wonderful opportunity I have as a Christian teacher, but in fact I see very little fruit for my labour. In any case, we cannot look for conversions. We must leave whatever influence we have to be brought to fruition by others, according to the will of God."

CHAPTER VI

School Worship

THOUGH the principal aim of this book is the discussion of religious education in the classroom, and hence with the scripture lesson, it must be remembered that in the maintained schools religious education also takes place at another point within the school day. The morning assembly in the vast majority of schools contains a period of worship, and the 1944 Education Act again makes specific mention of this. Most Christians have not concerned themselves with the formulation of reasons for daily worship in schools because to them, worship is the natural expression of their faith, and communal worship is an activity in which they join easily and happily. They would give specifically religious reasons for the practice of daily worship, for example that God has commanded it, that it is our duty and should be our delight, that it shows man at his highest and best, and that it depicts the right relation between man and his Creator.

However, there are queries and doubts as to the usefulness of daily worship in our schools today, so it is worth stating that in our view the continuance of this practice is highly desirable on broad educational grounds as well as for specifically Christian reasons. We hope that many whose point of view could not be called specifically Christian will also feel they can agree with the present position, for the reasons we shall now outline.

Morning assembly can be of great value in assisting the personal psychological development of schoolchildren, for it gives them a sense of belonging to a *community*. The warm, friendly, corporate spirit which characterises a community is contrasted by sociologists with the formal relations which exist in an *association*, which is merely a grouping of individuals who work together for some specific external need—for example the workers in a factory who are there to produce cars. But a community is a grouping the main aim of which is to further the personal well-being of its members in and through personal relationships. There is almost universal agreement that the school should aim to be a community, and since nothing fosters personal relations and a corporate 'spirit' like face-to-face meeting, it is essential that the members of this community should meet together regularly.

But the ritual of morning assembly is also useful in another way, in that it can become a uniquely valuable occasion for training in civilised group behaviour. At other times young people gather in a more disorganised way and their reactions are expressed at a more primitive level. Typical behaviour at a sporting event like a football match or at a pop music concert may provide a certain amount of katharsis, but mass participation of this kind could hardly be styled rational or civilised. But a reverent, thoughtful approach to a carefully planned activity of a serious nature is what is demanded for a worthwhile school assembly. This can be an initiation into the most fruitful and democratic way to participate in adult gatherings. 'Self-discipline' and 'decorum' are old-fashioned words, but they surely stand for attitudes which we should like to encourage in our children. Akin to this is also the respect for authority, the deference due to the speaker or the chairman or other person invested with authority by society. To understand the function of the head teacher at assembly, and the appropriate code of behaviour there, is for the child a first and valuable experience in this field.

The mention of authority may suggest that the assembly

ritual encourages a dangerous dominance on the part of the head teacher. However, the specifically religious content of assembly, in which acknowledgment is made of a greater Authority than pupil, teacher or school, saves assembly from developing into a breeding ground for tyranny. The head leads worship but he also worships with the school. A common dependence on, and subjection to, something above them all is expressed in hymns and prayer. In this way we are also linked with our own cultural tradition, which contains a national profession of religious faith.

Doubts have occasionally been expressed as to whether in the daily assembly worship in the fullest sense occurs at all. Some suggest that true collective worship of God can only be experienced in and through the full ritual of a church service. Others feel that only when those who take part fully commit themselves in humble adoration can worship be said to have taken place. It is, of course, impossible properly to assess the reality and quality of daily school worship, although its content and the way it is conducted may be commented upon. Morning services in maintained schools are undenominational in approach, but the hymns, prayers, Bible readings, and the short talk which may occasionally be given are usually clearly Christian in content. In every school there will be some who fully enter into the worship each day, some who are partly involved and some who merely attend.

We cannot, of course, force children to have religious experience, but it seems generally agreed that it is only right to allow them the opportunity to glimpse something of what the religious vision is. Our research has shown that one of the chief reasons why most parents, in all social areas, classes and occupation groups in the north-east, desire their children to attend the daily school assembly is this, that all children should have the chance to experience something of religious worship. Worship is in many ways the most favourable opportunity for religious insight, when we meditate on the great symbolic figures and stories, and join in the quiet communal ascription of worth and the dedication of ourselves to the highest that has been revealed to us.

Convinced Christians would speak of worship as the approach to God through His Son, Jesus Christ. And since our society as a whole has not cut adrift from Christianity, inevitably school assemblies will tend to be based upon the beliefs of Christianity. Professor Hirst points out that 'if (worship) is to be meaningful at all, it presupposes the acceptance of some beliefs including the belief that there is a point in praising and thanking and asking.''[1] There is no evidence of a widespread departure from the traditional Christian beliefs which make sense of these activities. Some parents however, would not be able to be so definite, yet would nonetheless never think of withdrawing their children. We shall never know how much daily school worship has meant to any individual child, although eloquent testimony to its value was noted by the Newsom Committee in its report, *Half Our Future*.[2]

That some—perhaps many—assemblies are lacking in vision, reverence, planning and a sense of 'the occasion' we are sadly aware. But the abuse of a ceremony does not necessarily imply that it should be abolished. The remainder of this chapter we shall devote to some of the possibilities of morning assembly and the experience of the men and women who have to lead it.

Today the subject of school worship is controversial. A small but very vocal minority is campaigning for its abolition from the school day. A much larger number, Christians as well as non-Christians, would like to see the compulsory provision in the 1944 Education Act either modified or removed altogether. Most schools still wish to retain the daily

---

[1] *op. cit.*, p. 14.
[2] H.M.S.O., 1963, p.58. The whole paragraph is worthy of note.

act of collective worship, despite the problems that many say this poses for them. The vast majority of parents are entirely satisfied with the present statutory arrangements. As we have just hinted, our research has shown that this contentment is no indifferent, unthinking acceptance of the existing *status quo*, but an attitude based on definite reasons. We found that well over half the parents who replied said that they believed in God and felt that school worship could help to foster in their children a consciousness of the divine. Other research has indicated that most children are happy enough to attend each day, though many are quick to criticise features of which they disapprove. The general situation, with interesting comments from teachers and children, is presented by Loukes in the chapter on compulsory worship in his *New Ground in Christian Education*, although some of his opinions and interpretations of quotations may fairly be questioned.

We asked a number of head teachers in maintained schools to comment on the morning assembly in their schools. All who replied agreed that the daily act of worship was an essential part of the religious education of their pupils. As one northern primary school headmistress stated: "Morning assembly forms a very important part in the communication of the Gospel." The secondary school heads were well aware that some of their pupils, usually the older ones, objected to being present or were indifferent to the proceedings. Most of the heads encouraged the open expression of such attitudes. Probably the majority of pupils are quite satisfied to go along with the usual arrangements. This seems to include most of the sceptical, especially if they have been allowed the satisfaction of indicating clearly what their own opinions are on the subject. In one school where the boys are expected to bring their Bibles with them to assembly in order to follow the passage being read, one agnostic sixth former objected to this practice. His headmaster explained that he was not demanding belief but insisting upon study. The boy found this argument acceptable. A Surrey headmaster acknowledges that there is more apathy today than twenty years ago. He quickly adds that "their need is correspondingly greater now". Nearly all would agree with him that on the whole the reaction of pupils to school worship is fair, and many of them, even the critical, truly value the experience.

What is morning assembly really like? A great variety of answers would be given to this question. A London headmistress says: "With junior children I try to make a balance between ritual, reverence and friendly informality, and this isn't always easy." In her school "the daily corporate act *starts* the day" and the children "almost without exception, enjoy it and enter in whole-heartedly". Like many headteachers in all types of school, she tries to encourage plenty of 'audience participation'. Another London primary school headmaster describes his school assembly as "a rather informal occasion, when we sing, laugh, exchange news and pray together. We always have a short talk, which is usually a two-way affair with questions and answers coming from both sides of the platform". A Midlands grammar school headmaster, however, conducts a very formal assembly, with plenty of variety in the readings and prayers (which has been appreciatively acknowledged by the pupils), the whole brief occasion being one of reverence and solemnity. In many schools now, children take a much more active part than they used to do, all the various year-groups being represented during the week. And the school in North Yorkshire which invites parents to join in the daily morning assembly with the children, is not alone in making such a perceptive and helpful gesture. Also members of staff other than the head often lead the worship or take some part in it. In one west country school twice a week a different master leads prayers on a theme of his choice. The themes taken by masters—with whose co-operation and ability we are here exceptionally fortunate—range from introducing hymns on a particular theme, prayers from history, Bible exposition, guided silence with music, 'lectures' on principles of conduct, education, politics, philosophy, etc., and one hundred and one in-genious ideas to capture attention and imagination, not infrequently using visual aids.

There are 'themes for the week', special series, readings from Christian writers as well as from the Bible, music, drama, mime, prayers and psalms composed by pupils, and very occasionally something excitingly creative and adven-turous like the mime of the Lord's Prayer described by Mary Bray in the journal *Learning for Living*.[1] In some schools children take one day's assembly entirely on their own and are usually left unhindered to organise as they choose. In one school, according to the religious knowledge master, one group wanted to have an assembly about the meeting be-tween the Archbishop of Canterbury and the Pope. Another group wanted the theme to be about unmarried mothers. Whether these topics were actually used, he did not say.

One headmaster said he had appointed an assembly com-mittee "to consider 'ways and means', but they have so far had little positive to offer—it's easier to criticise." A Suffolk head comments that

the 11–18 range is too vast to be suitable for every occasion and I should like to split up the school into more homo-geneous groups and smaller units from time to time. The difficulty is to find suitable alternative accommodation in our premises.

[1] Volume 4, no. 1. September, 1963.

Like others, at certain times this head has prayers for single
year groups, and "opportunities are taken from time to time
to follow up the theme of assembly in religious education
lessons".

In many schools, considerable pains are taken to ensure the
understanding and appreciation of what happens in school
worship, and when possible, feed-back is encouraged both
from the hall to the classroom, and from the classroom to
the assembly. One headmaster in the north-east adds:

> I am concerned to make this act of worship meaningful for
> the staff also. Unless something can overflow to them and
> into the life of the school in *all* departments if possible and
> result in a concern for each child, its problems and worries,
> I cannot be satisfied.

Another, contradicting some current pronouncements, says
"But the children on the whole are conservative and don't
like too much change." And a Lancashire headmaster speaks
for many when he writes:

> For better or worse I have eschewed gimmicks and efforts
> to rejuvenate Assembly, and concentrated on giving the
> impression that I regard it as important and meaningful, by
> taking trouble over the atmosphere in which it is conducted.
> Thus there is no talking on the way into or out of assembly,
> we get rid of all the notices before my entry—via the
> Deputy Head (though boys can see me waiting and listening
> at the door)—and only occasional things have my personal
> imprint. After all the notices we have our religious service
> which is fixed in form—opening prayer, hymn, reading,
> prayers, silence, grace, and the closing bars of the hymn
> repeated to 'round it off'—and masters and boys go out to
> a voluntary.

He has reorganised the seating with blocks of seats facing each other and his own position is off the stage and conveniently placed in the body of the hall.

This was primarily to avoid having a sixth form miles away downwind. Now no one is far from the centre, I am not unduly elevated, the staff is not worshipped (they sit with the boys), and the treble voices face one another and project a goodly noise at one another and at the broken reeds (or voices).

The challenge of school assembly is one that is being met with increasing understanding of the problems involved for both pupils and staff, with greater awareness of the needs, opinions and even comfort of all concerned. The unimaginative, casual, unfeeling, indifferent approach is still inflicted upon some schools. It is a reasonable hope that the present widespread discussion concerning daily school worship will lead to real improvements, where these are necessary. As the headmaster of the Lancashire grammar school concludes:

In the end, I'm afraid I think that it all comes back to me, largely, which is a solemn and sobering thought. I wish I didn't think this really. Nevertheless *what* is done is much less important than *how* it is done.

CHAPTER VII

The Way Ahead

THE FUTURE of religious education in our maintained schools is being widely questioned. The cries for reform are many and we have noted the main ones earlier in the book. It will be helpful now to summarise them. There is pressure to change the relevant clauses of the 1944 Education Act, in particular the compulsory provisions concerning daily school worship and the one weekly period (at least) of religious instruction. Many people are anxious to make radical changes in content. They draw attention to the existing Agreed Syllabuses and urge that revision of these be undertaken as soon as possible. A small number would like to see moral education separated from religious education and given its own special place in the school timetable. Changes in methods of teaching religious knowledge are also being demanded. The need for much improved conditions for the teacher of religious education is being more forcefully stated now. And the pupils themselves are reported to desire all kinds of alterations.

Such a ferment of interest and concern may well be healthy and promising, especially if those concerned to act consider all the various suggestions and points of view being put forward. Willingness to consider the necessity for change is essential at this time, although it does not always follow that change equals progress.

As regards compulsory daily worship and religious instruction, most schools seem to be satisfied with the present provisions of the Act. There has been no outcry of resentment from local education authorities or from the schools. It is probable that the great majority would continue with the present arrangements even if the compulsory clauses were removed from the Act. However, this is no argument in favour of abolishing those clauses. Ours is an officially Christian country. Our social structure and cultural history can be understood and appreciated properly, as we have said earlier, only in the light of some knowledge of the history and teachings of the Christian religion. Thus, to provide instruction in these teachings and regular opportunities for the experience of worship, which has such an important part to play in religious education, is essential to such understanding and appreciation. It is also fully consistent with democratic principles, given the safeguards which the Act includes for those parents who do not wish their children to attend school worship and religious instruction, and those teachers who, on grounds of conscience or principle, do not wish to teach religious knowledge. The Act ensures that parental rights are recognised and adequately preserved, and protects the teachers from unfair pressure or discrimination. It also ensures that the spiritual and moral education of children will not be completely neglected or overlooked.

The religious provisions of the Act continue to meet with the full approval of the vast majority of the nation's parents. Recent enquiries have revealed that over 90% are satisfied with the present arrangements. Our own research into parental attitudes to these provisions confirms this and reveals that parents in the north-east, at least, have many reasons for wishing their children to know about and understand Christianity and to attend daily school worship. In particular they feel that every child should have the opportunity of such teaching and worship because of their essential contribution to the development of character and personality and a responsible attitude to life and to others. These general reasons are frequently supported by specifically religious reasons.[1]

Since respect for the personality of every individual is a cardinal tenet of Christianity (even though, in some ages, Christians appear to have forgotten this), religious instruction as we have described it is consistent with the free development of each child. Christians would even argue that religious education is essential to a healthy child's development, because to deprive him of all knowledge of the great religious insights is to narrow disastrously the possible range of his vision, and to deny him access to the great ideals which have inspired past generations. The compulsory provisions of the Act thus ensure that the religious education of every child in our maintained schools shall not be neglected. They make it possible for all children to have instruction and the experience of worship essential to their full educational development, whether or not they later come to accept, or question, or deny the value of these. The provisions are therefore consistent with our beliefs as a Christian country. Without them, continued respect in education for the nature, the needs and the rights of every child could not be fully guaranteed.

There is, however, a widespread desire for changes in the Agreed Syllabuses. These have been under fire for some time and some revision is needed especially of aims and content. As we have noted before, many Agreed Syllabuses proclaim that the aim of religious education in the schools is the full commitment of the pupils to the Christian faith and way of life. It is the stated hope of many of them that the teaching according to the syllabus laid down will produce convinced Christians. Linked with this hope is another that the moral tone, indeed the whole character of the nation's life will be raised and strengthened. Teaching should be consciously

[1] See P. R. May "Why Parents Want Religion in School," in *Learning for Living*, Volume 6, No. 4, March, 1967, pp. 14–18, for a full account of this aspect of our research.

directed to these ends. We agree with many other writers that such aims go too far. It is not the religious knowledge teacher's task to produce Christians, or even simply men and women of good moral character, however much he may hope that his teaching may help to such ends. Such teachers must certainly put forward the evidence for Christian beliefs, but they should not be expected to ensure the acceptance of these beliefs. Their task is really to give such an understanding of religious belief, and particularly of the Christian faith—always bearing in mind the child's general development—as may lead to an appreciation of the Christian view of the world and of society and of the significance of Christian commitment. Seen in this light, religious education respects the integrity of the child and is quite open to argument and rejection. And such an approach, by definition, avoids the danger of indoctrination.

At all stages the nature and needs of the children should help to determine the approach adopted. Their views and questions should always be respected, but a wholly child-centred approach would be as unbalanced and inadequate as is the wholly subject-centred one practised in the past and encouraged by most Agreed Syllabuses. Proverbs, chapter 22 verse 6 makes the same point. We are to educate a child "in the way he should go". The need is to emphasise both the right standard at which to aim and the individual character and requirements of each pupil. Thus the content of religious instruction should be both Bible-centred and child-centred.[1] There is no fundamental inconsistency here. Agreed Syllabuses should be revised in accordance with this dual principle.

This leads on to the question of what should be included in the Agreed Syllabuses. In many there should be less emphasis on detailed material to be included in lessons and more

---

[1] For a more detailed consideration of this argument see P. R. May "The Bible and Children" in *Learning for Living*, Vol. 5, No. 3, January, 1966.

helpful guidance of teachers, encouraging them to adopt
individual, imaginative approaches wherever possible. We
emphasise again that biblical material must continue to have
a major place in the teaching at all levels, although it should
be selected and presented, as recent research has urged, in
ways which take full account of the pupils' needs and capacities as far as these can be evaluated. The Bible should be
regarded as the main source of material for general religious
education. One present difficulty is that we suffer from a
destructively critical approach to the Bible. Many teachers do
not know of the return to a more conservative position on the
part of recent biblical scholarship. The dismissal of much of
the Old Testament as a serious historical source, common in
the twenties and thirties, no longer finds many advocates,
for example. Also, since the habit of regular Bible reading in
the home declined, the problem of widespread ignorance of
what the Bible teaches, even among the educated sections of
the community, is a very real one. Thus the knowledge of a
teacher who is vaguely willing to assist in religious education
often leaves much to be desired.

For older children more specific emphasis should be placed
on ethics and the considering of moral problems. One advantage enjoyed by the religious knowledge teacher is that many
of the problems his subject deals with are real and actual, and
often within the grasp and experience of his pupils. This offers
the chance of a ready impact, whilst requiring sympathy and
tact in presentation. Account should also be taken of other
problems of modern society and of the application of the
Christian faith in modern life. Opportunities for social service,
for involvement in the life of the community, as a working
out of some of the 'insights' gained in class, should be sought
and seized. Lastly there is the question of comparative
religion, which some say should be given a larger share of time
in the religious knowledge syllabuses of older pupils. Whilst

admitting that the study of the major world religions can be
fascinating and may well be appropriate with fifth and sixth
formers, we agree with John Wilson that most children "do
not want to be taken for a conducted tour round a world
curiosity shop; they want to know whether any of the (different
religious and moral) beliefs are true."[1]

What of the pupils themselves? Most of them have little
background knowledge of the subject and of religious experience on which the teacher can build. Thus motivation is
often slight, and the reinforcement of learning well nigh
impossible. Nonetheless, most pupils, even the critical, are
interested in many aspects of the subject, and they are usually
quite eager to question and discuss. This is where a sound
knowledge of Biblical material gained in the earlier years
helps to make worthwhile discussion not only possible but
stimulating and meaningful. Recent research in educational
psychology has begun to shed more light on the way children
learn and the stages through which they pass on the road to
mature understanding. As regards their ideas about religion
and the development of religious understanding, much more
needs to be done. But the various capacities and levels of experience of children must never be ignored by the religious
knowledge teacher.

Conditions of work pose a great problem for many scripture
teachers. Many schools, whatever they may say in theory, in
fact do not take the religious education of their pupils seriously
enough. This is especially true in schools where academic
success is unduly stressed. English, mathematics, science and
languages are always emphasised, religious knowledge rarely, if
ever. Having only one period per week per class does not
help either, since pupils naturally tend to take more notice
of those subjects on which the school spends most time in
teaching and examining. Indeed, if, as a nation, we think

[1] *Aims in Education* p. 31.

religious knowledge so important that we legally require its provision in our schools, then to give the subject a fair time allocation and proper emphasis both in the schools and in teacher training is logical and right. Religious knowledge is also often the Cinderella subject when the question of money for books and equipment is raised. Many head-teachers are excellent here, being scrupulously fair and always helpful, but to equip every child in the school with all the books and aids needed is often much too expensive a business on a limited budget. Many teachers complain in particular that more and better books are needed, especially for younger children. Too many, they say, are badly designed and illustrated, deal with too large an area of knowledge, are condescending, and are not always intended for children to read themselves. Another problem is to get to know many of the pupils personally. This is often much more difficult for the religious knowledge teacher who sees his classes only once per week. Also relationships between home and school, so important in religious education, are often slight or non-existent. Closer contacts will be possible in the future, however, for those scripture teachers who assist with the work of school counselling. Many already help in this work and the growing interest of educationists generally in the problems of guidance suggests that this new office of school counsellor will become more common in our schools.

Perhaps the greatest problem in religious education today, however, is the shortage of supply of trained specialist teachers. There are still too many schools without the minimum requirement—one full-time religious knowledge specialist. This means that greater efforts must be made by all concerned with education to ensure an adequate future supply. The religious provisions of the 1944 Act themselves implicitly demand this. If we believe in the importance of religious education, then we should give it a more equal status with other subjects,

8

emphasise it more in the schools, encourage more pupils to study religious knowledge at 'O', 'A', and university levels, and seek to inform committed Christians generally of the urgency of the need. All teacher training establishments should take care to ensure that future religious knowledge specialists are fully trained in the methodology of their subject. They should be familiar with modern teaching aids and all the various methods of presenting their material. More opportunities should be made available for interested students and teachers who have not specialised in religious knowledge to study to gain appropriate qualifications. For practising teachers there should be many more regular in-service training schemes, and new information concerning teaching methods and the latest research findings should be made more readily accessible. Local seminars and short courses and conferences would also meet a widely felt need. The presence in every Local Education Authority of well qualified and widely experienced religious knowledge specialists as advisers of religious education would also be of great help to the scripture teachers of the area.

We are conscious that, as in the other subjects, there is inefficient and half-hearted teaching. Part of the problem here is that teachers with no proper qualifications in the subject are being allowed to take religious knowledge lessons. In some schools the only equipment is a set of battered copies of the Authorised Version. In others, scripture lessons consist of reading silently, copying and learning by heart. Notes are dictated by the teacher, questions and discussion are never invited, and the active co-operation and involvement of the pupils is never sought. Many children suffer disastrously under such dull instruction.

In the end, the way ahead in religious education in this country depends upon the Christian Church itself, upon the way it faces and fulfils its responsibilities. We have stressed that it is no part of the scripture teacher's job to evangelise. It would therefore be quite wrong to allow or encourage young people in our churches to train as teachers because they see the vision of a harvest of converts in the schools as a result of their work. Yet — other things being equal — clearly those with an 'inside knowledge' of religious experience will make the best teachers of the subject. A man without a love of music would make a poor job of teaching it. A person unable to appreciate poetry would be a feeble teacher of English literature. Similarly we ought to expect the vast majority of religious educators to be members of the Christian church and people to whom religion makes sense in personal experience. The ranks of the faithful should provide these teachers, even though we do not send them into the schools to recruit new members.

It is not unreasonable, therefore, to look to the Church for more committed men and women to teach religious knowledge, as well as for better and more up-to-date teaching of religion in Sunday schools and youth groups. If the Church speaks with an uncertain sound, few will respond to fill the many gaps in the schools. We fear that this is the case at present. The prevalence of a vague, inward-looking ecumenical temper in all denominations today tends to blur the clarity of the uncompromising New Testament gospel. The present shortage of religious knowledge teachers is hardly surprising in these circumstances. Ultimately the educational health of our schools will depend upon the spiritual health of our churches. And the spiritual health of our churches depends in the last resort upon the faithfulness of individual Christians and the preaching and teaching of the Word of God.

APPENDIX A

Research into Parental Attitudes

FROM TIME to time during this book reference has been made to our research, recently completed, into parental attitudes to the religious provisions of the 1944 Education Act. Parents have been questioned before, in a very general way, about these provisions, the best-known enquiry being the National Opinion Poll survey published in *New Society*.[1] Its findings included the facts that almost 80% of those questioned regarded Britain as a Christian country, and that 90% wished the present arrangements of religion in school to continue.

Our research in the north-east went into much greater detail and required more careful thought from the encouragingly large number of parents (over 53% of the 3,232 questionnaires sent out), from all social classes, areas and occupation groups, who answered our questions. As a matter of interest and because of their relevance to the subject of our book, we here include a few of our results.[2]

Over 96% of the 1,730 respondents said they wanted their children to know about and understand Christianity, and almost 83% said that it is part of the state day school's business to help the children in this.

Over 85% agreed with the statement that it is important for children in state schools to have religious instruction lessons, whilst 84% said that school worship is an important part of the daily life of state schools.

[1] Volume 5, No. 139, 27th May 1965, pp. 8—10.
[2] A detailed account of this research is given in the March—April 1967 edition of the *Durham Research Review*.

On the compulsory provisions of the Act, 77% want state schools to continue to be required by law to provide religious instruction lessons, and almost the same percentage (76·9%) want state schools to continue to be required by law to provide school worship. 17·6% opposed the compulsory provision of scripture lessons, and 18·9% that of worship.

However, over 90% want religious instruction lessons to be provided in school, even if the schools were no longer required to do so, and 88% want daily school worship to continue, even if the compulsory provision is abolished.

If the schools continue to provide religious instruction lessons and daily school worship, even though the law ceases to require them to do this, parents want their children to attend. The figures are over 92% concerning religious instruction lessons, and over 90% concerning worship.

Lastly the vast majority feel that half an hour a day of religious instruction, common in so many primary schools, is about right. In the secondary schools the majority favour rather more than just one period per week, and 14% would like five periods to be provided.

APPENDIX B

Qualifications

FULL-TIME specialists in religious education will always be needed, whatever changes in legislation may be contemplated over the next decade. University students thinking of teaching as a career do experience difficulties, however, as they decide how best to prepare themselves. Those students who are sure of their calling here will in all probability rightly opt for a university degree in Biblical Studies or Theology (Divinity). Despite the fact that the ultra-linguistic nature of these courses has come under criticism of late[1] and some changes seem desirable if a useful orientation towards the future teacher's needs is included in university studies, solid work at this level on Bible content, Church history, ethics and Christian apologetics is essential. Yet there is another way which is strongly to be commended.[2] This is the 'two-subject' teacher who has qualified at university degree level in two subjects—theology and one other. The increasing innovation and flexibility in degree courses at the modern universities make such a suggestion realistic for many more students than was possible fifteen years ago. But whether a single subject degree or some form of two-part or joint course is favoured, all graduates should spend a year at a university department of education. Academic degree courses are not intended to equip for school teaching, and in religious education especially, thoughtful consideration of classroom possibilities and techniques, training in metho-

[1] See *Religious Education* 1944—1984, *op. cit.*, chapters V and VI, and especially pp. 198—200.
[2] See the remarks of David Ayerst in *Religious Education* 1944—1984, pp. 70—72.

dology and skilled advice are essential—and a university Diploma in Education (or Graduate Certificate in Education) provides all these. Much harm can be done by the unskilled volunteer in any subject who proceeds straight into teaching from first degree; the wastage rate of such entrants to the profession is significantly high.[1] For the skilled teacher who is already a good general practitioner, but who feels the need for guided reading and a sounder knowledge of the academic background and content of religious knowledge, the London Certificate of Religious Knowledge or, at a higher level, the Diploma in Theology are useful qualifications. Both can be taken externally and in sections, by those working part-time. Secondment for a year's full-time study for the Diploma in Religious Education of London University is another excellent opportunity for practising teachers, and this course has proved both popular and extremely fruitful. In-service training of various kinds seems the only practicable way of meeting the teacher shortage in the future, unless the number of new entrants to the profession shows a substantial increase in the proportion of those desiring to specialise in religious education.

[1] See the statistics section of the Annual Report of the Department of Education and Science for any of the last five years, for instance.

APPENDIX C

The Plowden Report

Children and Their Primary Schools is the report of the Central
Advisory Council for Education (England) whose chairman
was Lady Plowden and which was published by the Stationery
Office early in 1967. It deals with all aspects of primary education, and recommended that the best age for transition to
secondary education would be 12 rather than 11.

In Chapter 17, "Aspects of the Curriculum", six pages are
devoted to religious education (pp. 203–209). After noting
disagreement among the Central Advisory Council itself on
the position of religious education in schools (six of the
twenty-five registered their views in a "Note of Reservation"
at the end of the report on pp. 489–492), the Report describes
the requirements of the 1944 Act, having remarked on the
widespread public support for these provisions (§§ 558–562).
In an interesting section on teachers' attitudes (§ 563) it is
noted the lowest estimate of teachers willing to give religious
education in any one primary school was 70%. Of those
actually engaged in such work less than one in five men and
less than one in ten women seemed reluctant or uninterested
in the task they were doing. In this informal survey by H.M.
Inspectors in 1963 and 1964, class teachers gave religious
instruction to their own classes in all but eight of the 163
primary schools visited.

The report goes on to admit certain difficulties in the
present position. The non-Christian teacher is tempted to
dishonesty or cynicism, and if he is honest his career prospects

are reduced; the non-Christian parent has to decide whether to ask for his child to be set apart and thus risk his feeling strange and isolated, or to let him attend religious education sessions and be taught what the parent holds to be untrue. Yet the main body of the report does not suggest any change, but rather a better information service to explain to parents and teachers what their rights are under the 1944 Act.

It is cautiously suggested that the daily act of worship might not necessarily retain its exclusively Christian chara-ter; it should be a focus of the school's common standards and values—an extremely important factor at the primary stage—and it should "illuminate personal relationships and introduce children to aesthetic and spiritual experience" (§ 571).

The report stresses that religious education should be given by the class teacher wherever possible and form a simple and positive introduction to religion. The committee does not wish children to be involved in religious controversy but believes (with the authors of this book) that judgments of truth or falsehood will only exceptionally be made by children of primary school age. Certainly they should not be taught to doubt before faith is established. If questioned, teachers must answer honestly and sincerely (§ 573).

The report notes the disquiet about the Agreed Syllabuses in many quarters, and welcomes research into children's con-ceptual development. The committee advocates the recasting (not the abolition) of the Agreed Syllabuses in line with this new knowledge. Teachers should be given the advantages of L.E.A. advisers in religious education (at present there are only four) and the opportunity for in-service training.

In general it may be said that the section on religious education is remarkably brief for a report of 427 pages in length, and not particularly radical in outlook. The note of reservation by the minority makes the following points: religious education taken seriously involves theology; theology is conceptually too difficult and too controversial for inclusion in the primary school curriculum; religion is neither desirable nor very effective as a basis for morals today; minority groups of teachers and parents find great difficulties with school religious education; the 'possibility of a choice between religious education or a secular course in moral and social education is at present an unrealistic option. (Two members of the committee, however, would like to see local bodies of teachers, parents and others set up to work out an alternative "Agreed Syllabus" of non-religious ethical teaching.) They conclude that religious education should cease to be an obligatory part of the curriculum and Assembly should be legally dissociated from the Act of Worship.

It will be seen from this outline that all the main issues raised in the Plowden Report, as well as the points made by the six dissentients, have been already discussed in various chapters of this book. No substantially new issues have arisen.

APPENDIX D

For Further Reading

1. On the religious factors in education in general

Christian Education in a Secular Society
W. R. Niblett   O.U.P.   1960
Education in Focus
E. C. Stanford   R.E.P.   1965
The Unity of Education
M. V. C. Jeffreys   R.E.P.   1966
Christianity in Education
F. H. Hilliard, etc.   Allen and Unwin 1966
Repair the Ruins
H. Blamires   G. Bles   1950

2. On the teaching of religion in schools

Teenage Religion
H. Loukes   S.C.M. Press   1961
Readiness for Religion
R. Goldman   Routledge and
                    Kegan Paul   1965
Religious Thinking and Religious Education
K. Howkins   Tyndale Press   1966
Changing Aims in Religious Education
E. Cox   Routledge and
                    Kegan Paul   1966